THE ETRUSCANS

HISTORY AND TREASURES OF AN ANCIENT CIVILIZATION

WHITE STAR PUBLISHERS

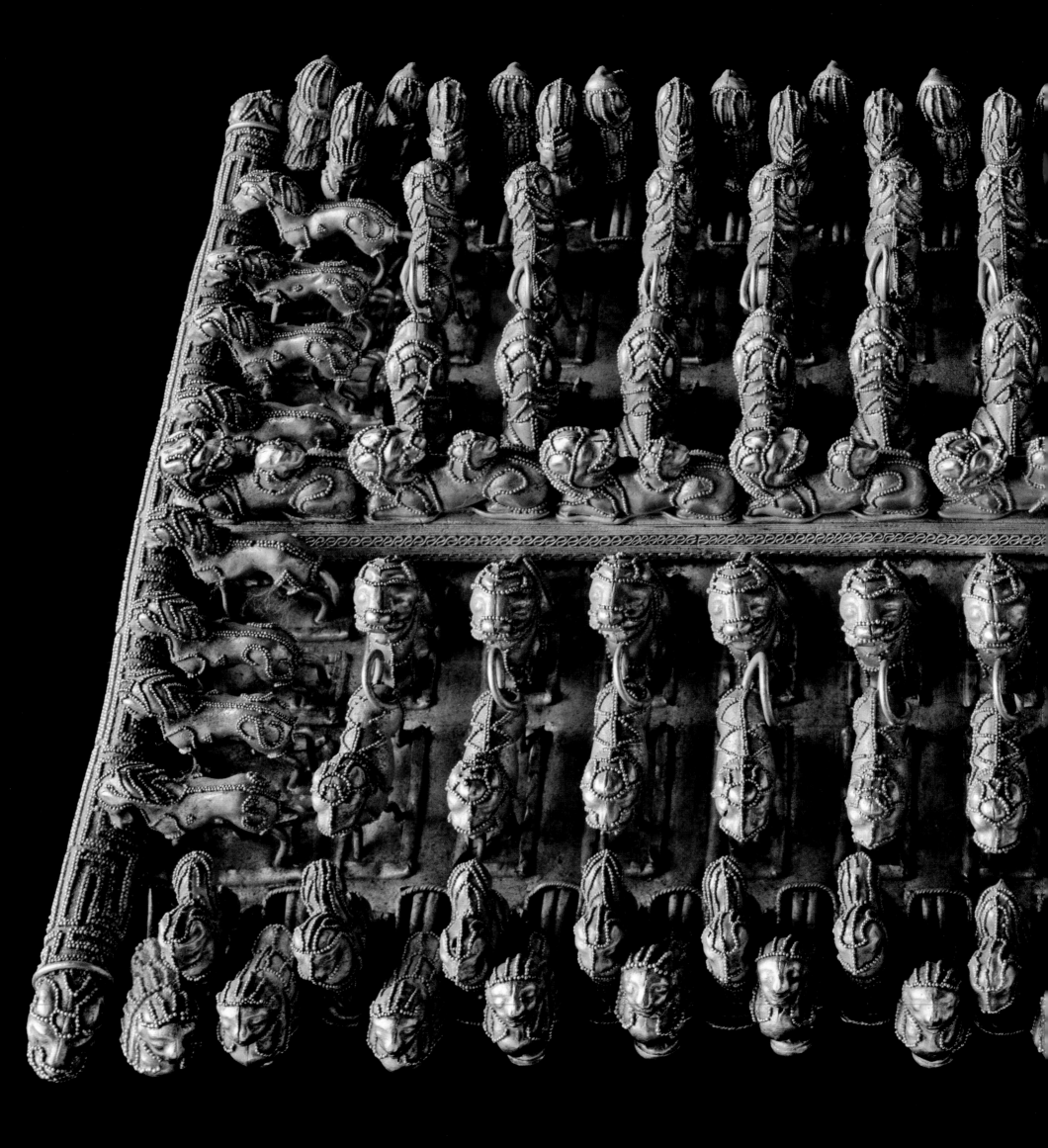

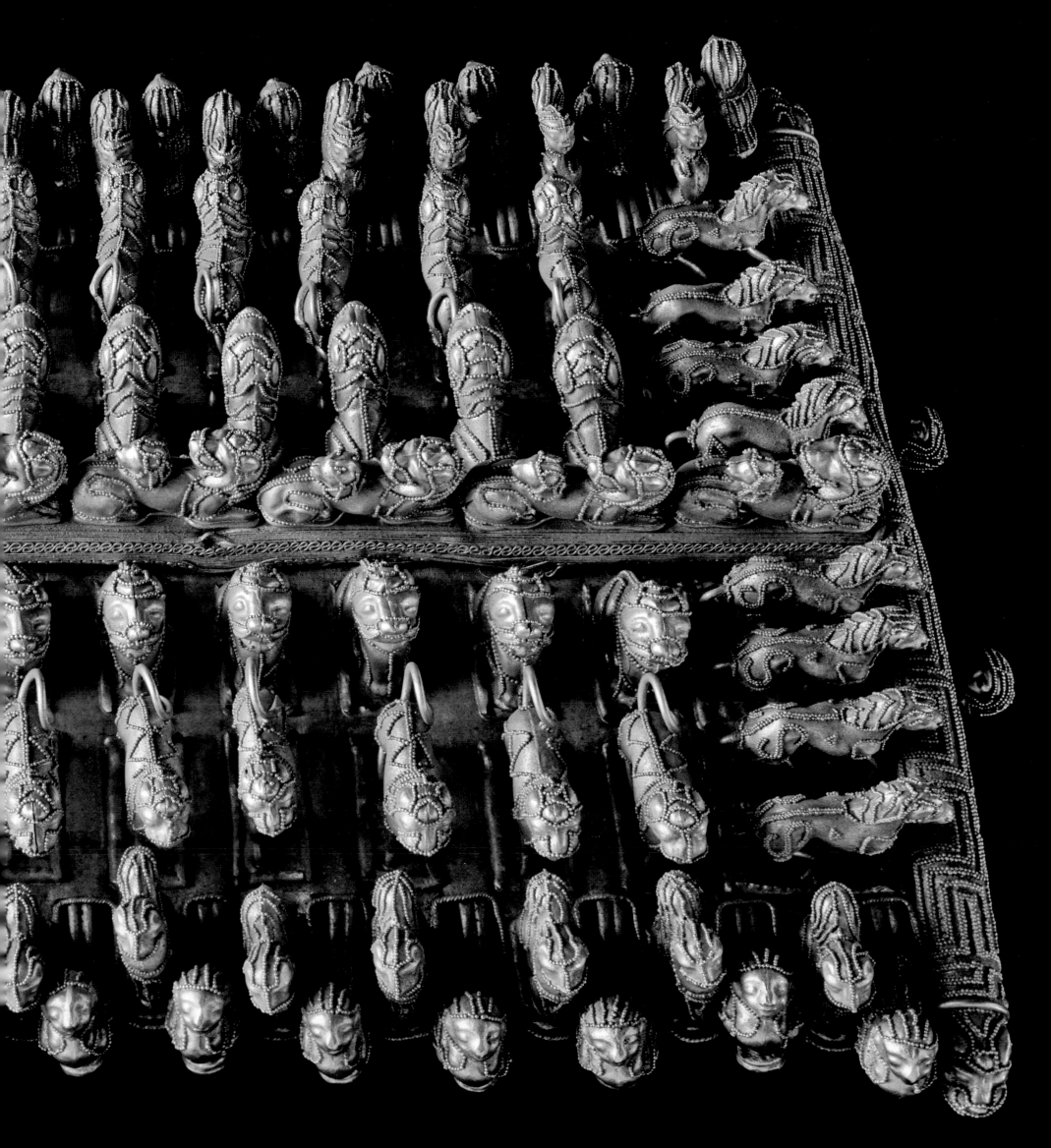

CHRONOLOGY
PAGE 12

THE ETRUSCANS AND ETRURIA
PAGE 20

BEFORE THE
ESTABLISHMENT OF CITIES:
THE VILLANOVAN CULTURE
PAGE 28

ARISTOCRATIC SOCIETY:
THE ORIENTALIZING CULTURE
PAGE 50

THE AGE OF EXPANSION:
THE URBAN CIVILIZATION
PAGE 90

THE PERIOD OF DECLINE:
CHANGE AND
ROMANIZATION
PAGE 168

INDEX - BIBLIOGRAPHY
PAGE 204

TEXT
ANTONELLA MAGAGNINI

EDITORIAL DIRECTION
VALERIA MANFERTO DE FABIANIS

COLLABORATING EDITOR
LAURA ACCOMAZZO
GIORGIO FERRERO

GRAPHIC DESIGN
PAOLA PIACCO

© 2008 White Star S.p.A.
Via Candido Sassone, 22/24
13100 Vercelli, Italy
www.whitestar.it

TRANSLATION: CATHERINE BOLTON

ISBN 978-88-544-0322-2

REPRINTS:
1 2 3 4 5 6   12 11 10 09 08

Color separation Fotomec, Turin
Printed in Cina

1 - THE LARGE GOLD DISK FIBULA IS FROM THE
REGOLINI-GALASSI TOMB IN CERVETERI (VATICAN
MUSEUMS, VATICAN CITY).

2-3 - THE BANQUET SCENE IS FRESCOED IN THE
TOMB OF THE LEOPARDS AT TARQUINIA.

4-5 - THE GOLD ORNAMENT WAS PART OF THE
FURNISHINGS OF THE BERNARDINI TOMB IN
PALESTRINA (VILLA GIULIA NATIONAL ETRUSCAN
MUSEUM, ROME).

6 - THIS LION'S HEAD IS PART OF THE BRONZE
CHIMERA, A VOTIVE OFFERING BY A PRINCE IN A
SUBURBAN SANCTUARY OF AREZZO
(ARCHAEOLOGICAL MUSEUM, AREZZO).

The Etruscans, their world and the external manifestations of their culture have long aroused curiosity, interest and the desire to learn more about them. The discovery of extraordinary monuments such as the Chimera of Arezzo, the statue of the Arringatore, the tumulus tomb of Castellina in Chianti, which is also depicted in a drawing attributed to Leonardo da Vinci, and artifacts with lengthy inscriptions reawakened an interest in the Etruscans as far back as the Renaissance, sparking bold conjectures. Two centuries later, in the 1700s, Italian culture was influenced by research and the collection of Etruscan archaeological material referred to as *etruscheria*. In this field, a series of works was published about the monuments and places in Etruria – which still attract enormous interest – although these works offered largely arbitrary and highly imaginative theories. During the 19th century, knowledge of Etruscan antiquities underwent sweeping revision due to the copious amount of material unearthed by the extensive archaeological campaigns that were conducted – accurately in some cases, less so in others – at the vast necropolises. At this point, the character of the studies moved from scholarly speculation to more solid methodological research, though various suppositions continued to fuel the idea of an "Etruscan mystery." Unfortunately, even today we find clichés that focus on "problems" or "mysteries" rather than on the real and extraordinary historical adventure of the Etruscans: the "problem of provenance" and thus of the unknown "origins" of this population; the "mystery of the language," considered indecipherable, and the "unexplainable" cultural development of a population notoriously devoted to luxury and moral laxity. Lastly, there is matter of the Etruscans' sudden and mysterious disappearance with the rise of the Roman civilization. Indeed, all of these topics have a timeless appeal. In reality, what has unquestionably contributed to the origin and popularity of this concentration of mysteries and conjectures is the diversity that set the Etruscans and their culture completely apart from coeval populations. The ancients perceived these differences during their own era, and this clearly emerges from the works of classical authors. For example, we can consider the descriptions of the Etruscans provided by Dionysius of Halicarnassus, a Greek historian who lived in Rome during the Augustan Age. In his monumental work entitled *Roman Antiquities*, he devoted Book I to the history of Italic populations, also discussing the Etruscans. The Etruscans fascinated the historian so much that he discussed them separately, focusing on their diversity. He also noted that this population was far more ancient than others in the area, and that their language and lifestyle was completely different. This diversity and uniqueness is clearly confirmed by archaeological documentation. Rather than citing "mysteries," Etruscan studies explain these differences through a well-grounded reconstruction of the historical context and of the economic, social, political and artistic aspects of this population. According to this reconstruction, the Etruscan culture originated and developed over an extremely long period of time, from the 9th to the 2nd century BC.

Consequently, we can study the Etruscans and reconstruct their civilization using various resources: literary sources, i.e., the set of knowledge and information handed down to us by ancient writers; epigraphic sources, meaning documents written in Etruscan on various types of materials; and archaeological sources, which represent the most substantial category.

8 - The gold disk earring is decorated with a series of concentric motifs composed of tiny balls and floral elements, made using filigree and granulation techniques, and set with contrasting blue glass paste (British Museum, London).

9 - The head of the god Hermes is part of the lavish decoration on the sanctuary of Portonaccio in Veii. A masterpiece of Etruscan terracotta sculpture, it dates back to the late 6th century BC (Villa Giulia National Etruscan Museum, Rome).

With regard to the literary sources, it is important to note that, given the complete lack of direct evidence of an original Etruscan literary tradition, we can rely only on information handed down to us by Greek and Roman writers. Nevertheless, attentive reading of the works of the latter allows us to surmise that they were familiar with Etruscan sources, which in turn may have drawn on the private documentation of aristocratic families. For example, in writing a twenty-book work about the Etruscans, of which we know only the title, *Tyrrenikà*, Emperor Claudius was undoubtedly assisted by his wife Urgulanilla, who descended from a noble Etruscan family and gave him to access the archives of notables.

The Greek writers include not only Dionysius of Halicarnassus (late 1st century BC) but also Herodotus, Polybius, Diodorus Siculus, Strabo and Plutarch, all of whom lived in different eras. With regard to the Etruscans and their culture, the Greek authors commented chiefly on differences in customs, lifestyle and language. Moreover, in their accounts of the historical events involving the Etruscans, their descriptions often have a clearly anti-Etruscan slant.

Likewise, when we consider the works of the Roman writers – for example, Livy, Virgil, Pliny and Tacitus – we must bear in mind that the purpose of their accounts was to provide a positive representation of the history of Rome. Consequently, their interest in the Etruscans served this purpose and, as such, the historical and political events of Etruria and the Etruscan population were often marginal, if not disregarded entirely. While bearing these aspects in mind, the important information handed down to us by the literary sources is fundamental for the correct historical reconstruction of the Etruscan civilization.

A completely different contribution comes from the study of epigraphic sources, as they represent documentary evidence left by the Etruscans in their own tongue. These sources are fundamental, as they are the most substantial set of evidence written in a language spoken in ancient Italy aside from Latin, Greek and Phoenician-Punic. However, most of the more than 7000 inscriptions that have survived to our day are brief and related to funerary practices. As a result, the inscriptions can help us only in part in reconstructing the aspects of Etruscan history and society.

Lastly, the archaeological sources are highly significant, as each one has specific informative elements that can be gleaned through a correct methodological approach. Advances in studies and archaeological excavations, conducted using increasingly sophisticated scientific research methods, have yielded substantial information on dwellings, places of worship, production sites and necropolises, which are now better defined and accurate with regard to evidence of the material culture. Additional information comes from studies of bones – human and animal – and paleobotanical remains.

The correct analysis of these valuable sources of knowledge, which can fruitfully be compared, combined with the study of literary and epigraphic sources, allows us to reconstruct crafts and artwork, consumption and trade, as well as the daily life, economic activities, religion and social structure (roles, ranks classes and social differences) of the Etruscan civilization.

The goal of this book is to sketch out its development from the 9th to the 2nd century BC, highlighting the unique aspects of a civilization that played a fundamental role in ancient Mediterranean history.

11 - THIS REPOUSSÉ GOLD PLAQUETTE, WHICH WAS USED TO DECORATE CLOTHING OR BELTS, IS EMBELLISHED WITH A WINGED FEMALE FIGURE CREATED USING THE GRANULATION TECHNIQUE. IT WAS MADE IN SOUTHERN ETRURIA IN THE SECOND HALF OF THE 7TH CENTURY BC. THE OBJECT WAS FOUND IN THE TOMB OF THE DOLI IN CERVETERI (VILLA GIULIA NATIONAL ETRUSCAN MUSEUM, ROME).

DANUBE

LAKE BALATON

LAKE NEUCHÂTEL

LAKE GENEVA

LAKE MAGGIORE

LAKE COMO

LAKE GARDA

ADIGE

PIAVE

TAGLIAMENTO

DRAVA

SAVA

PO

ESTE

ADRIA

SPINA

MARZABOTTO

FELSINA

VERUCCHIO

ARNO

MASSALIA

LIGURIAN

SEA

TIBER

VOLTERRA

MURLO

BROLIO

FERMO

PERUGIA

ADRIATIC

SEA

POPULONIA

TODI

VETULONIA

CHIUSI

ROSELLE

ORVIETO

TALAMONE

MARSILIANA

BISENZIO

VULCI

ACQUAROSSA

GRAVISCA

TARQUINIA

PYRGI

VEII

CERVETERI

ROME

ALALIA

PALESTRINA

SATRICUM

TYRRHENIAN

SEA

CAPUA

CUMAE

PONTECAGNANO

IONIAN

SEA

SYRACUSE

14-15 - The Sarcophagus of the Spouses is an enormous cinerary urn made in the shape of a *kline*. The couple, depicted in a banquet scene, shows supple and elegant modeling. Made in a Caeretan workshop, it dates back to the late 6th century BC (Villa Giulia National Etruscan Museum, Rome).

16-17 - The monumental tumuli built for the aristocracy stand out in this aerial view of the Cerveteri necropolis.

18-19 - The scene on this cippus, or funerary marker, depicts a stage with three judges observing athletic competitions (Archaeological Museum, Palermo).

VILLANOVAN CULTURE
(9th-8th century BC)

The Villanovan culture developed in Etruria at the beginning of the 9th century BC and led to the foundation of the great Etruscan communities. This culture is distinguished by the unification of the population in settlements established on large tufa plateaus and hillsides, and by the adoption of cremation, with the use of biconical impasto urns to hold the ashes of the dead, which were placed in a well. At the end of the 9th century BC, transformations took place, with the use of interment along with cremation and richer tomb furnishings. At the beginning of the 8th century BC, with the foundation of Pithekoussai, the communities of the Tyrrhenian region of central Italy had contact with Greek seamen from Euboea, from whom not only acquired goods but also gained technological and artistic knowledge, and new models. In the second half of the 8th century BC, a hierarchical society became established in the proto-urban centers, in which the nascent aristocracy was able to plan and organize various activities.

ORIENTALIZING CULTURE
(8th-6th century BC)

The Orientalizing culture was introduced to Etruria during the last two decades of the 8th century BC. This culture was characterized by the arrival of luxury products from the Near East, which were purchased thanks to the economic potential of the emerging aristocracies. In the 7th century BC, precious imitation items also became part of the numerous assets accumulated by the aristocracies. These goods were destined for burials that had reached levels of astonishing wealth and complex rituality. Between about 630 and 580, princes focused their demand for splendor on the construction of enormous residences. Writing was fully acquired as an aristocratic cultural element during this period.

THE URBAN CIVILIZATION
(6th-5th century BC)

At the beginning of the 6th century BC, the rise of urban forms implied the sweeping political and urban reorganization of the great Etruscan centers, which were modeled after the Greek polis. Intense building activity was accompanied by great reclamation work that also involved the countryside, leading to substantial redevelopment of the forms of exploitation of agricultural resources. These changes also occurred with increased mining of resources, for which more systematic production methods were implemented. The dodecapolis was established during this period. This league, composed of the 12 dominant cities of Etruria proper, was complemented by cities that developed in Padana and Campanian Etruria as a result of sweeping expansion and the occupation of new territories. Territorial expansion was accompanied by intense maritime trading that, through a series of routes fanning out across the Tyrrhenian Sea, led to the creation and consolidation of a broad sphere of influence as important as that of Carthage. In the 6th century BC, the arrival of goods and merchants from eastern Greece (Ionia) led to aristocracy's adoption of lifestyles revolving around luxury and the characteristics of the opulent societies of Asia Minor. Moreover, starting in the second half of the 6th century the massive presence of pottery produced in Athens – a medium that conveyed Greek iconographies and the knowledge connected with them – powerfully accelerated the acculturation process of the ruling élite classes, leaving a decisive mark on the Etruscan mentality and culture. By the end of this century Etruria was a complex political and economic entity that was fully a part of the Mediterranean scenario. At the beginning of the 5th century BC, the international situation changed. In 480 the Syracusans' victory over the Carthaginians at Himera and of the Greeks over the Persians at Salamis allowed the Greeks to gain power in the Tyrrhenian Sea, conflicting with Etruscan interests. In 474 at Cuma and in 453–452 in the waters off the island of Elba, the Etruscan fleet faced two heavy defeats. The impact of these losses was evident above all in the great centers of Southern Etruria, with a decline in sea trade and decreased imports. Nevertheless, the economic deficit of these territories was offset by the prosperity of the cities in the central and northern areas, to which the center of political and economic power thus shifted.

THE PERIOD OF DECLINE
(4th-2nd century BC)

After Veii fell to the Romans in 396, the cities of Southern Etruria attempted to organize a coordinated reaction against Rome, starting with Tarquinii, which in 358 commenced a long war that did not end until 351, when a forty-year truce was signed. In this changing political scenario, the aristocracy had to consolidate its power in the face of strong social and economic tension, adopting new ideological instruments and altering the rapport between the large cities and the surrounding territory. Based on this new type of political and territorial organization, some of the cities of Southern Etruria significantly revived their economic activities, promoting trade and craftsmanship, and producing in much large quantities. With the turn of the 3rd century BC, the line of resistance and offensive against Rome moved to the cities of the inland and northern areas, whose oligarchies managed to ally the Samnites, the Umbri and even the Gauls as a way to reopen hostilities. Nevertheless, the harsh, bloody battles were unsuccessful, with defeats at Sentinum in 295 and near Lake Vadimo in 283. From this moment on, like the cities of Southern Etruria before them, those of Inland Etruria – no longer united – were defeated one by one. The Etruscan political, economic and social structure gradually dissolved, as it had become inadequate to deal with the new economic and military dynamics of Italy and the Mediterranean. Less than two decades after the capture of Veii, Rome managed to erase Etruscan power from the peninsula's political map.

1

THE ETRUSCANS
AND ETRURIA

Origins and Language
page 22

The Etruscans: A Population
of Pre-Roman Italy
page 24

Etruria: Environment and Resources
page 25

The Underpinnings of the Development
of the Etruscan Civilization
page 26

The "origin" of the Etruscans was one of the issues that most intrigued ancient writers and it has long piqued the interests of modern scholars. The subject was first examined by the Greek historian Dionysius of Halicarnassus who, in his *Roman Antiquities*, reported and discussed the various theories known to him. The most important one was the theory of the Greek historian Herodotus (5th century BC) who posited that the Tyrrhenians (in Greek the Etruscans were known as *Tyrrhenoi* or *Tyrsenoi*) had descended from the Lydians, who lived in an inland region of Asia Minor. According to Herodotus, due to an extended period of famine, a group of Lydians, led by the king's son Tyrrhenus, left their homeland and reached the land of the Umbri, where they settled and took the name of their leader. Hellanicus of Lesbos, a contemporary of Herodotus, also indicated that they came from overseas. He identified the Etruscans as the Pelasgians, a legendary population of wanderers from the Peloponnesus who, driven out by the Greeks, reached the mouth of the Po and descended the Italian peninsula to Cortona, where they called themselves Tyrrhenians. Dionysius of Halicarnassus rejected these theories of

the eastern origin of the Etruscans, citing them instead as a native population of very ancient origins that did not resemble any other culture on the Italian peninsula in either language or customs. The scholars of the 19th and early 20th centuries who investigated this "fascinating problem" traced their studies either to Herodotus' idea of an eastern provenance (this was the most popular theory), to Dionysius' "native" theory, or to a third theory whereby the Etruscan and Italic populations had arrived from the north, crossing the Alps. The watershed in the problem of the "origins" of the Etruscans came in the 1940s with the studies conducted by Massimo Pallottino, the father of Etruscan studies in Italy. Focusing on the tangible concept of "formation" rather than the abstract one of "origins" or "provenance," he emphasized that the various issues adopted until then actually had many points in common and did not contradict each other, as long as one did not wish to demonstrate that the Etruscans were a unitary entity that had already formed in a very ancient age, either locally or in distant lands. The process of the formation and ethnolinguistic definition of the Etruscan population must be considered the result of a progressive genesis dating back to the Bronze Age or even early, to which various elements – Italian, Eastern and European – contributed and matured in Etruria.

Like their "origins," the Etruscans' language was also the subject of observations and analyses that, particularly in the past, shrouded it in mystery. Based on scientific studies, however, there are absolutely no grounds for such an enigma. Etruscan is a dead language, as are Latin and Ancient Greek. Unlike them, however, it did not leave any legacy, as all information has been lost. The only way to learn about it is thus by studying written evidence that is not particularly substantial from a qualitative standpoint. Nevertheless, the interpretation of written texts has been the starting point for different methods of investigation. As a result, our knowledge of the Etruscan language is not paltry by any means, as we have discovered many aspects of the vowel and consonant systems, the existence of cases (as in Latin and Greek) and numerous elements related to syntax. We also have substantial information concerning vocabulary. There are approximately 8000 comprehensible words, most of which do not have an Indo-European etymology. However, there are a few words with Indo-European roots; another component is constituted by loanwords from the Greek, Latin and Italic languages, dating to the historical era. Therefore, we know many terms indicating kinship, such as *apa* father, *ati* mother, *clan* child. We are also familiar with words about the state and society – *zilath* magistrate, *lauti* freedman, *spur* city – as well as words about the divine and funerary world, such as *ais* god, *cepen* priest, *suthi* tomb, *mutna* urn. We know the names of objects, plants and animals – *thafna* statue, *malena* mirror, *spanti* plate, *leu* lion, *eleva* oil – and verbs such as to do, to give, to live and to die. Though with a few uncertainties, we also know the terms for the numbers from one to nine. There are approximately 7500 texts that, depending on their scope, the type of medium on which they were found (vases, sarcophagi) and their discovery site (tombs, sanctuaries or dwellings) have provided us with a large number of words. More importantly, they have also allowed us to investigate the very structure of the language, despite the fact that, based on the state of the art in research, for the most part we can grasp the general meaning of the text but cannot come up with a true translation, which has been possible only in the cases – unfortunately quite rare – in which bilingual texts have been found. Thus, Etruscan is not a mysterious tongue but a language with a different structure, one that is isolated with respect to coeval languages. Nevertheless, new findings and studies are making it increasingly comprehensible.

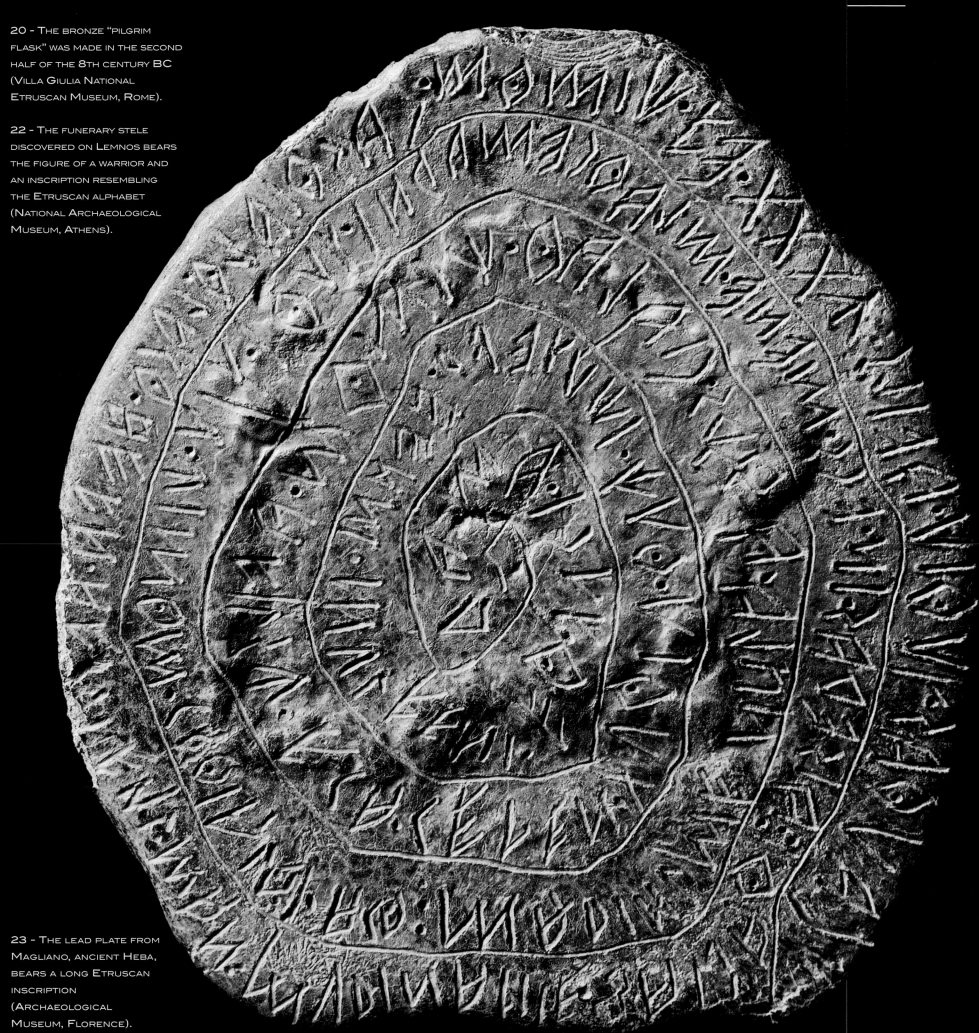

20 - The bronze "pilgrim flask" was made in the second half of the 8th century BC (Villa Giulia National Etruscan Museum, Rome).

22 - The funerary stele discovered on Lemnos bears the figure of a warrior and an inscription resembling the Etruscan alphabet (National Archaeological Museum, Athens).

23 - The lead plate from Magliano, ancient Heba, bears a long Etruscan inscription (Archaeological Museum, Florence).

THE ETRUSCANS: A POPULATION OF PRE-ROMAN ITALY

In order to grasp the formation process of the Etruscan civilization, the rise of its powerful aristocracy, its economic underpinnings, forms of trade, military organization, unique social and political structure, extraordinary arts and crafts, and – lastly – its decline, we must bear in mind that the scenario for all of this was pre-Roman Italy. This term is used to refer to the Italian peninsula before its political, juridical, linguistic and cultural unification under Rome. Before the ancient peninsula was unified by the Romans and Augustus divided it into administrative divisions in 7 BC, creating 11 regions distinguished by traditional geographical and ethnic names, it was split up into different populations that had different origins, languages and cultures, and were marked by extremely varied levels of progress. This multiform scenario mirrored an equally multifaceted environmental and cultural picture that went far back in time, to the periods of Italian prehistory and protohistory, when the processes that formed the civilizations of ancient Italy commenced. The Italian peninsula was a place that, because of its conformation and position, encouraged human settlement in very ancient times, even when great climatic variations profoundly influenced the environment. It is a territory composed of nearly 5000 miles (8050 km) of coastline, numerous mountain chains, broad plains and varied landscapes, with countless species of flora and fauna, as well as a wide variety of resources. One of its most distinctive features is the fact that it is set in the middle of the Mediterranean Sea, thus making it open to outside contact. All of these factors contributed to forming an extremely varied set of cultures with distinctive features not only on a chronological level, but also in the different geographical areas. In order to reconstruct such a complex scenario, research – which has becoming increasingly interdisciplinary in scope – has turned to an extensive, albeit uneven, set of data, above all concerning the material culture, i.e., the large quantity of artifacts, some of which easier to decipher than others, that a civilization produces, accumulates and leaves behind. Examined alongside information regarding anthropological and environmental aspects, the artifacts have revealed the chronological course of events, correlated with a comprehensive picture of the economic activities, social organization, and ritual and symbolic aspects that distinguished the various cultures of Italian prehistory and protohistory. For the oldest phase, or the Stone Age, this long path has been divided into three periods: Paleolithic, Mesolithic and Neolithic. The Neolithic, datable between about 5500 and 3000 BC, represents one of the most significant moments in human evolution. Indeed, it left a profound and lasting mark on the history of the Italian peninsula through the extraordinary changes that

took place: the transition from an economy based on hunting and gathering to a production economy revolving around farming and raising livestock, the production of pottery and tools, changes in the social organization, and cultural and ideological aspects. The Stone Age was followed by the Metal Age, in which humans discovered this precious resource and began to use it. This too generated revolutionary transformations in man's relationship with the environment, coupled with profound changes in the territorial, economic and social structure. This long period has conventionally been divided into three stages, named after the different metals or alloys whose circulation distinguished them. They span a timeframe from the 3rd to the 5th millennium BC. It is important to note that different methodological approaches and the new chronologies that have been devised, based on radiocarbon measurements and dendrochronology, have led to different views on datings that are not unanimously accepted. The Copper Age (or Eneolithic), which lasted from approximately 3000 BC to 2000 BC, was followed by the Bronze Age (named after this alloy of copper and tin). In turn, the Bronze Age is divided into three main periods: the Early Bronze Age (19th–17th century BC), the Middle Bronze Age (16th–14th century BC) and the Late Bronze Age that, in turn, is divided into a recent phase (13th–mid-12th century BC) and a final phase (11th–10th century BC). The period ends with the Iron Age (9th–8th century BC). During the Metal Age, Italy was an extraordinary kaleidoscope of cultural facies that has yielded so much information that scholars have been able to sketch out rather detailed scenarios of the cultures that characterized the different parts of the peninsula. It has been noted that, starting above all in the Bronze Age, the communities were organized into villages that relied on significant collective planning, tied to the exploitation of agricultural resources, thanks also to the use of bronze tools. These implements were much more efficient than the stone and copper tools of the preceding periods. Scholars have also noted that, for their settlements, these communities began to choose strategic sites that allowed them to monitor the territory and make the most of its resources. The biggest centers, which demonstrated an advanced organization, came into contact with Mediterranean trade, and for many communities this sparked enormous progress in the acculturation process. Large settlements formed in the Iron Age, developing throughout the peninsula, albeit in different ways. They were marked by a highly evolved level of planning, accompanied by equally developed socioeconomic structures. This rich and varied scenario ultimately served as the backdrop for the fully formed cultures distinctive of pre-Roman Italy, and one of these was the Etruscan civilization.

To define the territory of pre-Roman Italy occupied by the Etruscans (*Rasenna*, as they referred to themselves, *Tyrrhenoi* or *Tyrsenoi* in Greek, and *Etrusci* or *Tusci* in Latin), we can start with the area occupied by *Regio VII*, according to Augustus' administrative division. In modern geographical terms, this corresponds to Tuscany, northern Lazio (Roman Latium) and the western portion of Umbria. With the exception of the latter, these areas are situated along the Tyrrhenian, the sea that was named after none other than the Etruscans or *Tyrrhenoi*. This large area of the peninsula still has environments and landscapes distinguished by great morphological differences, as well as a wide variety and distribution of agricultural, forest and mineral resources. It is likely that this scenario closely resembled the ancient one, despite the fact that, over the centuries, humans have unquestionably left their mark, above all as far as the landscape is concerned. In Etruscan studies, this area, which is referred to as Etruria proper, is divided into three districts: Northern Etruria, Inland Etruria and Southern Etruria.

Northern Etruria, set between the Albegna River to the south and the Arno to the north, has broad hilly areas, plains along its numerous river valleys, and a coastal area that is level in some areas and has lagoons in others, with two deep natural inlets near Talamone and Populonia. The Tuscan islands, Elba first and foremost, are part of this district, and the promontory of Piombino forms a natural bridge between the islands and the mainland. The most distinctive feature of this area is the fact that it has numerous ore districts that are rich in copper, iron, lead, tin and silver. These districts include those around Massa Marittima, Madonna di Campiglio, Elba and Montee Amiata. Inland Etruria, which corresponds to the broad river valleys of the Chiana and the upper Tiber, is instead distinguished by vast level areas that extend around Lake Trasimene, the largest body of water in central Italy. The entire area, with rolling hills, boasts clay deposits that yield top-quality material for pottery. Southern Etruria, between the Tiber to the south and the Albegna to the north, has volcanic terrains with broad tufa plateaus, referred to as "promontory plateaus," that are bounded by plains, waterways and three rather large lakes, Bracciano, Vico and Bolsena. These lakes formed in the extinct craters of enormous volcanoes. Most of the coastline is distinguished by long beaches and coastal lagoons. Southern Etruria – particularly the area of the Tolfa Mountains – is rich in ores such as copper, iron, lead and silver, as well as alum, although it seems that the latter was not exploited until the Renaissance. In all three districts, the more mountainous areas were covered with dense woodlands that provided wood and game. The numerous lakes and rivers ensured an abundant supply of water and fish, while also providing inland communication routes and, near the mouths, excellent landing places and natural ports. The coastal areas and lagoons also yielded another very important resource, salt, which was used extensively even in very ancient times to preserve food and tan hides. However, the two mainstays of Etruria's economy from the very beginning were agricultural and mineral resources. Not only did they permit permanent occupation of the territory and influence settlement patterns, but the increasingly profitable exploitation of resources gradually led to burgeoning production activities and trade.

While agricultural resources fully satisfied the dietary needs of the individual communities in a subsistence economy, the intensification of farming and crop specialization transformed the system into a surplus economy, in which excess products were destined for exportation. Likewise, even in very ancient times, mineral resources attracted foreign traders to the communities that controlled them. This allowed these settlements to acquire artifacts as well as technologies, customs and ideologies, and to develop the intense international trade that was yet another cornerstone of the Etruscan economy. As a result, this population came to occupy a leading position in the Mediterranean scenario in pre-Roman times.

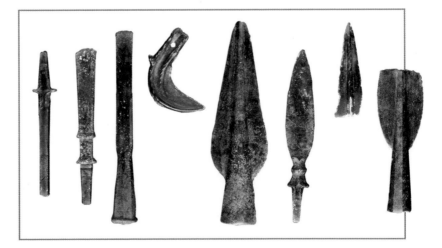

24 - THE SET OF DOUBLE AXES AND THE BRONZE FIBULA ARE FROM A CACHE DISCOVERED NEAR LIMONE, WHICH YIELDED OBJECTS FROM THE LATE 10TH AND EARLY 9TH CENTURIES BC (CIVIC MUSEUM, LIVORNO).

25 - THE OBJECTS FROM THE LIMONE CACHE INCLUDED BRONZE WEAPONS AND TOOLS: PROJECTILE POINTS, A SICKLE AND A SET OF CHISELS FROM THE LATE 10TH AND EARLY 9TH CENTURIES BC (CIVIC MUSEUM, LIVORNO).

THE UNDERPINNINGS OF THE DEVELOPMENT OF THE ETRUSCAN CIVILIZATION

Now that we have taken a look at pre-Roman Italy and examined the territory of Etruria and its resources, we must examine some of the aspects of the phases in the formation of the Etruscan civilization, without which it would be impossible to arrive at a correct historical reconstruction. Scholars generally agree that the cultural processes that ended in the Early Iron Age with the rise of the Etruscan *nomen* (nation) must have commenced in the Bronze Age, and specifically in the middle period (16th–14th centuries BC). This was a period in which central Italy was distinguished by various cultural facies that were culturally and historically uniform, and were connected with the Apennine civilization. The Apennine culture, which was theorized in the 1950s by the archaeologist Salvatore Puglisi, is named after the area in which a series of communities along this mountain ridge developed. Their subsistence was dependent on raising livestock, with transhumance activity and, as has recently been established, also on an agricultural economy. As far as Etruria is concerned, archaeological documentation, mainly from the southern district, has been obtained from settlements as well as necropolises, such as Luni sul Mignone and Crostoletto di Lamone in the Fiora river valley. In terms of population, there was a general reorganization with an increase in settlements situated on high ground and covering up to 12 or 13 acres (4.8 to 5.2 hectares), pertaining to groups of several dozen people. The settlements were built at even distances along communication routes. Among them, we can identify several centers that play a dominant role; they were characterized by large elongated structures that have been dubbed "long houses," which were discovered at Luni sul Mignone.

The subsistence economy was supplemented by agriculture, the cultivation of cereals and legumes, and animal husbandry connected with the practice of transhumance, as demonstrated by the campsites and seasonal shelters that have been unearthed in areas such as Monte Amiata. Hand-molded impasto pottery was produced on a family level and was characterized by the creation of "open" forms such as bowls and cups, connected with a semi-liquid diet and the processing of milk. The incised decoration presented banded motifs with meanders and spirals that evoke wood carvings. The bronze implements, particularly axes and daggers, must have been produced by craftsmen who traveled to the different communities, as demonstrated by the spread of a certain type of axe throughout Italy. The discovery of loom weights and the extraordinary finding of cotton thread and bits of wool near the hearth of a dwelling demonstrate that weaving

and spinning were practiced. As far as the funerary aspect is concerned, we can note that during this period both interment and cremation were used, with a certain level of variety in the type of burial. Nonetheless, burials were always accompanied by vases and bronze objects. In some cases, such as the tumuli with collective depositions, the furnishings were especially rich, as a way to emphasize the fact that the deceased had a different status in the group. The evidence we have noted regarding settlements concentrated on high ground, the existence of ruling dominant centers that had differentiated structures within the settlements, and the appearance of elements of distinction in rituals and tomb furnishings would indicates that, within the communities, there were dominant groups that centrally coordinated the various activities.

It seems that they can be connected with a new settlement strategy that characterized the later phase, conventionally referred to as the Sub-Apennine facies, in the Late Bronze Age (13th–12th century BC). The progressive movement of settlements to sites that had natural defenses led to a decrease in the number of settlements, accompanied by an increase in population density. Moreover, the presence of ruling groups in the Sub-Apennine communities is confirmed by the fact that several settlements, such as the one at Monte Rovello, have larger-than-average structures, and their tomb furnishings include spears and swords, clearly indicating a class of armed men. During this period, the increase in economic activities – farming as well as the exploitation of mineral resources – was matched by an increase in the number and quality of crafts, characterized not only by the production of hand-molded impasto pottery, whose functional forms were distinguished by handles surmounted by a wide variety of sculptural elements, but also by the substantial production of bronze objects. For the latter, the discovery of crucibles and casting molds demonstrates that new workmanship techniques had been adopted.

A fascinating element that underscores the central role of Tyrrhenian Italy in the Mediterranean scenario involves contacts with the Aegean area. This is proven by the Mycenaean potsherds found at Monte Rovello and the discovery at Mycenae, in the House of the Oil Merchant, of a mold for a type of axe that is unquestionably Sub-Apennine in style. The Mycenaean merchants, contemporaries of the princes who destroyed Troy, were attracted by Etruria's rich mineral resources, and their seafaring laid the foundations for the intense international trade that was destined to play a key role in the formation and development of the Etruscan civilization in the periods that followed. So far we have discussed the phases in which the Etruscan civilization was gradually formed. However, the regional differences that were the direct forerunners of the cultures that developed during the Iron Age became evident along the Tyrrhenian coast of central Italy during the Final Bronze Age (12th–10th centuries BC), in a period that has been named the Proto-Villanovan. During this period, there was a rapid transformation process marked by a highly differentiated population structure, in which settlements on high ground, on plateaus, around lakes and along the coast flourished and grew significantly. The settlements – notably Luni, Monte Rovello, San Giovenale, Sorgenti della Nova, Allumiere and Tolfa, in the Tolfa Mountains – occupied areas ranging from just over an acre to 25-30 acres, populated by 100 to 200 individuals. The spaces were organized into functional areas distinguished by various activities. The ones occupied by dwellings had isolated huts or groups of huts, and were larger in size. Moreover, the construction of defensive works indicates that there may have been conflict between communities. The larger number of settlements and population growth went hand in hand with increased production, due to the exploitation of a wide range of agricultural and mineral resources, and accelerated trade among the various settlements, which is confirmed by their higher concentration near natural communication routes.

In terms of funerary rituals, the Proto-Villanovan necropolises were distinguished by cremation. The remains of the deceased were placed in biconical urns closed by a bowl or, in rare cases, in "hut urns." The urns were then placed in *pozzi*, or pits, that were protected by a tufa lid or lined with stone slabs.

The objects found in burials, for example in the tombs at the necropolis of Poggio la Pozza at Allumiere, located in the inland area of Cerveteri (ancient Caere), clearly show that crafts continued to be characterized by hand-molded impasto pottery, in which open forms were supplemented by biconical

vases with incised zigzag motifs and hemispherical sculptural forms. Nevertheless, the most interesting aspect involves the production of bronze artifacts, which developed significantly during this period, with the production of weapons, personal ornaments, particularly prestigious vessels, and implements with such a distinctive local appearance that it seems likely that metalworking artisans were part of the community. This explosion in the demand for metal artifacts is indicated above all by the discovery of numerous hoards. In most cases, these hoards of intact or fragmentary bronze objects were buried outside residential areas and were probably connected with artisan activities. Their formation – with a stock of raw materials, items to be repaired and articles intended for the market – can be explained based on the specific characteristics of the objects pertaining to them. For example, the hoard found at Coste del Marano, in the area of the Tolfa Mountains, must have been a full-fledged treasure, a collection of luxury objects hidden close to a nearby dwelling. Composed of 148 bronze items, nearly all of which intact, it had ornamental items such as fibulae, brooches and pendants, as well as items with a special function – possibly for rituals – such as an axe and a shovel, and extremely valuable items such as repoussé vessels.

Studies of the accoutrements, the arrangement of the necropolises and the differentiation of certain residential structures suggest a social organization based on kinship units with the intentional distinction of certain members of the community. Moreover, the presence of imported objects indicates complex, dynamic and, in some cases, long-distance trade linking Etruria with Latium, Sicily, Sardinia and the Aegean area.

These settlements and populations were well organized. In terms of funerary rituals as well as crafts, their characteristics are closely connected with those of the Early Iron Age. In the subsequent Villanovan period, they would distinguish the period in which the great Etruscan communities emerged.

27 - THE DRAWING SHOWS WHAT THE LONG HOUSES DISCOVERED AT THE BRONZE AGE ARCHAEOLOGICAL SITE OF LUNI SUL MIGNONE MAY HAVE LOOKED LIKE.

BEFORE THE ESTABLISHMENT OF CITIES: THE VILLANOVAN CULTURE

The Rise of the Etruscan *Nomen*:
the Large Proto-Urban Centers
page 30

The Impact of the Greek World:
Contact, Presence and Production
page 42

Transformation and Changes:
Funerary Ideologies, Social Structures
and the Circulation of Goods

The Rise of the Aristocracy:
Cultural Models and Emerging Elites
page 46

THE RISE OF THE ETRUSCAN NOMEN: THE LARGE PROTO-URBAN CENTERS

With the transition to the Iron Age, toward the beginning of the 9th century or possibly the last decades of the 10th century BC, the Villanovan culture developed in a vaster area than Etruria proper, chronologically paralleling what the ancient sources have handed down to us regarding the origin of the Etruscan *nomen* or nation.

The term "Villanovan" was coined in the mid-1800s by Giovanni Gozzadini, a Bologna archaeologist who used it to define the funerary manifestations that characterized the 179 cremation tombs he fortuitously discovered in Villanova, a town in the province of Bologna. This term has unfortunately caused a great deal of confusion, above all in cases in which the expression "Villanovan" was given an ethnic significance that juxtaposed the "Villanovan population" with the "Etruscan population." Therefore, it is important to clarify that the terms "Villanovan" and "Villanovan culture" refer to a system of customs representing the typical expression of the material culture of the Early Iron Age that developed in the area that was historically Etruscan.

Based on the enormous amount of data that this extraordinary cultural facies has yielded, we can divide it into three periods: an initial period up to approximately 820 BC; an intermediate period from about 820 to 770 BC, and a third period – known as the Evolved Villanovan – between about 770 and 720 BC. Moreover, it is possible to pinpoint the vast area in which it was manifested, which included not only Etruria proper (Tyrrhenian Villanovan) but also Emilia and Romagna (Emilia and Romagnola Villanovan), Marche (Fermo Villanovan), Campania, in the Salerno and Sala Consilina areas (Salerno Villanovan), and Lucania, in the Diano valley.

The most distinctive and revolutionary aspect of the Villanovan period was the radical change in the type of settlement and territorial organization, as previous settlements were abandoned and the population merged to form larger centers. It has been estimated that this extraordinary concentration process reached a ratio of 20 to 1. In other words,

20 Proto-Villanovan villages merged to form a single Villanovan center. The other aspect typical of the Villanovan culture that, as opposed to the former, had significant points of contact with the preceding Proto-Villanovan facies, was the adoption of cremation, with the use of biconical vases to hold the ashes and the presence of tomb furnishings. These two elements – territorial layout and cremation – distinguish the Villanovan from other Iron Age cultures in ancient Italy.

These Villanovan settlements, which would later develop into large Etruscan cities such as Veii, Cerveteri, Tarquinia and

29 - THE BRONZE HELMET (FIRST HALF OF THE 8TH CENTURY BC) IS COMPOSED OF A HEADPIECE WITH THREE CYLINDRICAL ELEMENTS ON THE SIDES AND ROWS OF BOSSES THAT ARE REPEATED ON THE TALL CREST (BRITISH MUSEUM, LONDON).

30-31 - SECTIONS OF THE HUT URN ARE DECORATED IN BRONZE (PRIVATE COLLECTION).

31 - THE TERRACOTTA HUT URN IS FROM VULCI (VILLA GIULIA NATIONAL ETRUSCAN MUSEUM, ROME).

Vulci, are thus defined as "proto-urban," a term that evokes the importance of the territorial restructuring dynamics that commenced in the Iron Age and were powerfully linked with the subsequent phases of the Etruscan civilization.

Vast tufa plateaus with natural defenses on three sides and hilly areas were chosen for these new settlements, which covered approximately 370 to 440 acres (150 to 180 hectares) and were occupied by several hundred individuals. The sites were situated close to important natural overland and fluvial communication routes, as we can still see today if we trace what would later become the Via Aurelia, which passed through the proto-urban centers of Cerveteri, Tarquinia, Vulci, Marsiliana, Roselle, Vetulonia and Populonia. Likewise, the proto-urban towns of Veii, Orvieto (ancient Volsinii) and Chiusi (ancient Clusium), to name just a few examples, were near the route that would later become the Via Cassia and the Tiber River. With the exception of Populonia, directly along the coast, the sites were also chosen close to coastal landing places and connected with the areas that exploited agricultural and mineral resources.

Information from the few settlements in which methodical research has been conducted can be used to reconstruct the dwellings and internal organization of the villages. The results of these studies can be integrated with information from co-eval cinerary urns shaped like huts, which gives us an idea of the elevation and roofs of the huts. For example, at the Villanovan settlement of Calvario, near Tarquinia, analysis of the imprints left in the soil indicates that the huts varied greatly in size and layout – round, oval or rectangular – and that they had large round holes inside to insert posts to support the roof. The presence of a hearth is suggested by findings of the remains of embers and ash on the ground.

As demonstrated by the rare findings of clay fragments with traces of straw, the façade was composed of a lattice of reeds and branches covered with sun-dried clay to make it more solid and waterproof. As we can see from the specimens of hut urns from Tarquinia, Vulci and Vetulonia, these buildings had one or two windows, with a door on the short side. The outside walls of the urns were richly decorated with incised geometric motifs that would conceivably also have embellished on dwellings, as is the case even today at certain South African villages. They had a testudinate roof – in other words, shaped like a tortoise shell, or with four slopes – and an opening on the front to ventilate the interior and vent smoke. It was supported by a framework of four posts that crossed at the top. In the most prestigious huts, they may have ended in a bird's-head motif that served a decorative purpose but was also designed to protect the dwelling.

Reconstruction of the internal layout of the Villanovan villages appears to be more difficult. They completely covered the enormous plateaus on which they were built, but the dwellings were alternated with clearings that were probably used to grow crops or for other functions. The areas were not evenly spaced, which may indicate sections that pertained to distinct kinship groups composed of several families. It is important to point out that this radical change in the population and layout of the territory, with the abandonment of villages and the integration of populations at new locations, could not have occurred without political planning by ruling groups that had already formed within the communities of Proto-Villanovan Etruria, which evidently preferred territorial reorganization to conflict.

The necropolises – about which we have learned a great deal thanks to archaeological research – were established outside the vast residential areas.

As we embark on our in-depth examination of the Etruscan civilization, it is interesting to note that study data from necropolises played a key role in reconstructing this culture. Given the complex rituals that accompanied them, burials provide a "snapshot" of the social group that established them. By studying them we can reconstruct numerous aspects, ranging from indications about the deceased (gender, age, social status), the structure of the community, arts and crafts, and even contact and exchanges with other communities, offering us insight into lifestyles and ideological aspects.

In the 9th century BC, burials distinguished by the exclusive use of cremation were represented by cylindrical wells excavated in virgin soil. In Northern Etruria, Emilia and Romagna, the wells were lined with rocks or stone slabs positioned to form a parallelepiped container protecting the ossuary. In Southern Etruria, however, the burials were sometimes protected by tufa or nenfro (a type of volcanic stone) containers: tombs discovered in Volterra (ancient Volaterrae) and Tarquinia eloquently exemplify these different methods.

Externally, burials were marked by the lids of their containers, but some also had slabs (a fascinating one found in Bologna is carved with the schematic representation of a hut) or hut-shaped stone *cippi* (cylindrical sepulchral marker) such as those of a tomb in Tarquinia.

In most cases, the impasto urn that held the ashes of the dead was composed of a biconical vase that was richly decorated with geometric motifs incised using a comb-like tool. As was the case in the Proto-Villanovan period, for some burials a hut-shaped urn, also intricately decorated, was used in place of a biconical vessel, as in the case of Tomb 45 at Poggio Selciatello in Tarquinia.

The biconical urns were covered with a stone or terracotta helmet and had one or two handles. However, it has been noted that if there was second handle, it was intentionally broken for ritual purposes.

The furnishings of these older tombs were extremely limited, with rare vases and equally rare metal objects inside the urn. Fibulae and razors were used for male burials, and fibulae, hair spirals and loom weights for female burials. The burials thus seem to have been distinguished by egalitarianism, distinguished only the gender of the deceased. However, if we look at certain tomb furnishings, such as those of three tombs at the necropolis of Poggio Selciatello, we can grasp several elements of differentiation. In the first one – a male burial – a clay helmet with a peaked top, covering the biconical vase in place of the usual stone, clearly indicates that the deceased had been a warrior. The 29 reels and 4 loom weights placed in the urn of the deceased from the second tomb emphasized the art of spinning: among women, spinners had the same high status as warriors among men. Lastly, given its rareness the richly decorated hut urn from the third burial was attributed to a figure who had enjoyed a special position during his lifetime.

Consequently, it seems that in this early phase egalitarian society was moving toward a diversification of roles.

The study of furnishings also points to a sharp increase in crafts. With regard to pottery made from hand-molded impasto, which was used to create cups and biconical forms embellished with a repertoire of geometric images rendered with comb-like tools, it has been theorized that family production was complemented by the presence of craftsmen's shops, as the stylistic and technical affinities shared by a series of artifacts would seem to suggest.

The origin of the proto-urban centers coincided with the occupation of new lands to cultivate, encouraged by the use of new agricultural implements made of iron, reflecting the ability to mine and work this metal. Paleobotanical and animal remains demonstrate an overall improvement in the cultivation of crops, particularly cereals, as well as animal husbandry, which came to play an important role in the population's subsistence economy thanks to a greater focus on selection processes.

33 LEFT - THIS OBJECT WAS PART OF MALE TOMB FURNISHINGS FROM TARQUINIA. THE IMPASTO VASE WITH AN ASYMMETRICAL OPENING (ASKOS), IN THE SHAPE OF A BULL, WAS MADE IN THE SECOND HALF OF THE 9TH CENTURY BC (ARCHAEOLOGICAL MUSEUM, FLORENCE).

33 RIGHT - THE BICONICAL VASE FROM VOLTERRA (9TH CENTURY BC), WHICH HAS A SINGLE HANDLE, WAS USED TO HOLD THE ASHES OF THE DEAD. IT IS DECORATED WITH BANDS OF LINES AND HAD A BOWL AS A LID (ARCHAEOLOGICAL MUSEUM, VOLTERRA).

TRANSFORMATION AND CHANGES: FUNERARY IDEOLOGIES, SOCIAL STRUCTURES AND THE CIRCULATION OF GOODS

In the late 9th century BC, during the period that is referred to as "intermediate," Etruria's proto-urban centers underwent significant changes that can be gleaned from the information obtained from tomb furnishings. These accoutrements are distinguished by the presence of various objects that not only contribute to a historical reconstruction, but are also significant in terms of both quality and number.

Though the territorial organization remained the same, it is clear that three fundamental changes took place: the use of interment along with cremation; generally richer furnishings found in tombs that held both cremated and interred remains; and the circulation of goods and dynamic trade relations among the various Villanovan communities as well as other cultures.

The first transformation involved funerary rituals. Alongside cremation burials, accompanied by richer accoutrements with respect to the Early Villanovan period, inhumation also began to appear at necropolises: the dead – fully clothed – were placed supine in pits, with a substantial array of furnishings composed of personal ornaments, pottery, weapons and various types of objects.

Alongside this difference in the type of funerary ritual, it is interesting to observe that the funerary structures used in this phase had different features. Consequently, we have a much more diversified picture with respect to the preceding period: the pit was covered with stones or square blocks; tufa enclosures or circles of stones were used to indicate the tombs on the ground level; and the burials were organized in groups in specific sections of the necropolis. An aspect that later became particularly significant can be seen in the singular presence of burial chambers with one or more depositions at Populonia, long predating findings from other necropolises of Etruria and protohistoric Italy.

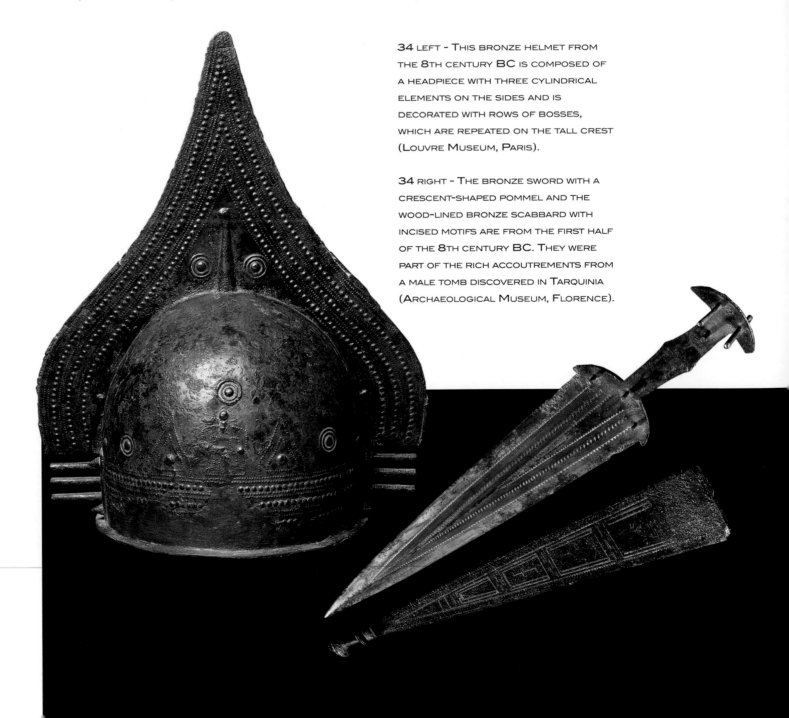

34 LEFT - THIS BRONZE HELMET FROM THE 8TH CENTURY BC IS COMPOSED OF A HEADPIECE WITH THREE CYLINDRICAL ELEMENTS ON THE SIDES AND IS DECORATED WITH ROWS OF BOSSES, WHICH ARE REPEATED ON THE TALL CREST (LOUVRE MUSEUM, PARIS).

34 RIGHT - THE BRONZE SWORD WITH A CRESCENT-SHAPED POMMEL AND THE WOOD-LINED BRONZE SCABBARD WITH INCISED MOTIFS ARE FROM THE FIRST HALF OF THE 8TH CENTURY BC. THEY WERE PART OF THE RICH ACCOUTREMENTS FROM A MALE TOMB DISCOVERED IN TARQUINIA (ARCHAEOLOGICAL MUSEUM, FLORENCE).

As we have already noted, the second transformation is evident in the general enrichment of the tomb furnishings for both cremation and inhumation burials. Two cremation burials of armed men, discovered in Tarquinia, are highly significant. The rich association of bronze artifacts unquestionably signals the warrior status of the dead, which were accompanied by their weapons, helmets, lances and swords, as well as a razor. The accoutrements included sets of bits and cheekpieces for horses, and even miniature chariots indicating the ownership or use of a transport chariot. The latter were also present in female burials.

The hunting scene on the scabbard is especially fascinating, as it is the oldest documentation of an activity that distinguished the emerging élite classes. Along with banquets, games and processions, over the years hunting would become one of the hallmarks of the Etruscan *principes*.

35 LEFT - THIS BRONZE LUNATE RAZOR FROM VETULONIA DATES BACK TO THE 9TH CENTURY BC. ITS CAST HANDLE HAS A RING, IN ORDER TO HANG IT UP, AND BOTH SIDES OF THE BLADE ARE DECORATED WITH SAWTOOTH PATTERN (ARCHAEOLOGICAL MUSEUM, GROSSETO).

35 RIGHT - THIS BURIAL SET WAS COMPOSED OF AN IMPASTO DOLIO (JAR) CONTAINING AN OSSUARY WITH A BOWL-SHAPED LID. THESE OBJECTS, ALONG WITH THE FURNISHINGS, WERE DEPOSITED INSIDE A STONE CIST. DISCOVERED IN VOLTERRA, THIS TOMB DATES BACK TO THE 8TH CENTURY BC (ARCHAEOLOGICAL MUSEUM, VOLTERRA).

36 - THIS RARE OBJECT IS A GOLD FIBULA WITH A LONG PIN SET IN A DISK-SHAPED ELEMENT INCISED WITH GEOMETRIC MOTIFS. THIS PRECIOUS ORNAMENT WAS USED TO FASTEN CLOTHING. IT IS FROM THE CAVALUPO NECROPOLIS AND DATES TO THE SECOND HALF OF THE 9TH CENTURY BC (VILLA GIULIA NATIONAL ETRUSCAN MUSEUM, ROME).

36-37 - THE REPOUSSÉ NECKLACE IS COMPOSED OF THREE GOLD-LEAF DISKS DECORATED WITH GEOMETRIC MOTIFS AND CONNECTED BY SMALL AMBER CYLINDERS. THE OBJECT WAS FOUND IN A FEMALE TOMB AT BISENZIO AND DATES TO THE 8TH CENTURY BC (VILLA GIULIA NATIONAL ETRUSCAN MUSEUM, ROME).

During this phase, female burials were also characterized by numerous personal ornaments, including large lozenge-shaped belts made of bronze sheets with incised and repoussé decorations, numerous fibulae of various styles, and hair spirals. Jewelry included necklaces with bone and vitreous-paste beads. As we have already noted, the weapons found in male burials as status indicators were paralleled by spinning instruments in female burials, as spinning was considered a prestigious activity for women with a high social standing. An example of this can be seen from a female tomb from Tarquinia, in which the spindle was associated with a disk fibula covered in amber and bone, and an impasto jug with a very elaborate shape, underscoring the status of the deceased. All the burials – male and female – had large num-bers of ceramic vessels made of a beautiful brown impasto. They were made in a wide variety of functional forms, some of which quite distinctive, such as boat-shaped vessels like the one found in Tarquinia, with a prow in the form of a bird's head to which bronze eyes must originally have been attached. One explanation for this enormous change in the enrichment of tomb furnishings is the desire of certain members of the community to flaunt their wealth and status, but at the same time also it also reflects the increased complexity of the funerary ritual itself. As we will see, in the period that followed the ritual seems to have included a banquet. In these furnishings, this custom is documented by a miniature bronze table that symbolized the meal, such as the one found at a tomb in Tarquinia.

48 - THIS BICONICAL VASE, MADE OF
SHEET BRONZE, WAS USED TO HOLD THE
ASHES OF THE DEAD. ITS CRAFTSMANSHIP
IS QUITE INTERESTING: THE SHOULDERS
AND LID BEAR A SERIES OF FIGURINES
WITH HEADPIECES, SHIELDS AND LANCES
THAT ARE DANCING AROUND A
MONSTROUS FIGURE, WHICH MAY
REPRESENT ONE OF THE GODS OF THE
UNDERWORLD. THE OBJECT DATES BACK
TO THE 8TH CENTURY BC, FROM
BISENZIO (VILLA GIULIA NATIONAL
ETRUSCAN MUSEUM, ROME).

49 - This rare hut urn is made of sheet bronze decorated with geometric motifs. The ends of the roof beams are decorated with figures of birds, and on one side of the urn there is a door that can be opened. It is from a tomb at Vulci and dates to the 8th century BC (Villa Giulia National Etruscan Museum, Rome).

54-55 - This valuable bronze vessel has two mobile handles and a basin decorated with concentric bands, with incised floral motifs, animals and a hunting scene. The artifact was found at the Tarquinia saltpans and dates back to the 7th century BC (Louvre Museum, Paris).

55 - This picture shows the mounting of a bronze lebes composed of a double male head with a Phrygian cap bearing a ring. The object was found at a Vetulonia burial site known as the Circle of the Cauldrons and was made by Syrian craftsmen in the first half of the 7th century BC (Archaeological Museum, Florence).

62 LEFT - THE SILVER POURING VESSEL (OINOCHOE), WITH A DOUBLE HANDLE WHOSE BASE ENDS IN A GOLD-LEAF PALMETTE, WAS PART OF THE MOST IMPORTANT ORIENTALIZING COMPLEX EVER DISCOVERED FROM ETRURIA: THE REGOLINI-GALASSI TOMB AT CERVETERI. IT IS FROM THE COAST OF ASIA MINOR OR CYPRUS, AND WAS MADE BETWEEN THE LATE 8TH AND EARLY 7TH CENTURIES BC (VATICAN MUSEUMS, VATICAN CITY).

62 RIGHT - THIS PRECIOUS OBJECT IS A GOLD-LEAF CUP (KOTYLE). IT HAS TWO HANDLES, EACH OF WHICH IS DECORATED WITH A PAIR OF SPHINXES. ITS FORM RESEMBLES THAT OF GREEK KOTYLAI, BUT IT WAS PROBABLY MADE IN ETRURIA IN THE FIRST HALF OF THE 7TH CENTURY BC. THIS ARTIFACT IS FROM THE BERNARDINI TOMB DISCOVERED IN PALESTRINA, ANCIENT PRAENESTE (VILLA GIULIA NATIONAL ETRUSCAN MUSEUM, ROME).

63 - THIS PRECIOUS
SPHERICAL CAULDRON IS
MADE OF GILDED SILVER.
AROUND THE EDGE, IT IS
DECORATED WITH SIX
SERPENTS CREATED IN THE
ROUND; THE SURFACE
FEATURES FOUR REPOUSSÉ
AND ENGRAVED FRIEZES
SEPARATED BY A BRAID
MOTIF. THE ARTIFACT
PRESENTS SEVERAL
DIFFERENT SCENES, FRAMED
BY PALM TREES, WITH FOOT
SOLDIERS, HORSEMEN,
FARMERS AT WORK AND
HUNTERS. THE CAULDRON,
MADE IN CYPRUS, IS FROM
THE BERNARDINI TOMB AT
PALESTRINA (VILLA GIULIA
NATIONAL ETRUSCAN
MUSEUM, ROME).

64 - THE OUTERMOST FRIEZE OF THIS GILDED SILVER PATER DEPICTS A ROYAL HUNTING SCENE. THE INNER ONE PORTRAYS A PROCESSION OF HORSES AND BIRDS IN FLIGHT, AND THE CENTRAL ONE SHOWS AN EGYPTIAN FIGURE STRIKING AN ENEMY. THE CUP, MADE IN CYPRUS, IS FROM THE BERNARDINI TOMB (VILLA GIULIA NATIONAL ETRUSCAN MUSEUM, ROME).

65 - THIS GILDED GOLD CUP FROM THE REGOLINI-GALASSI TOMB WAS MADE IN CYPRUS OR POSSIBLY IN ETRURIA, BUT IS THE WORK OF PHOENICIAN CRAFTSMEN (VATICAN MUSEUMS, VATICAN CITY).

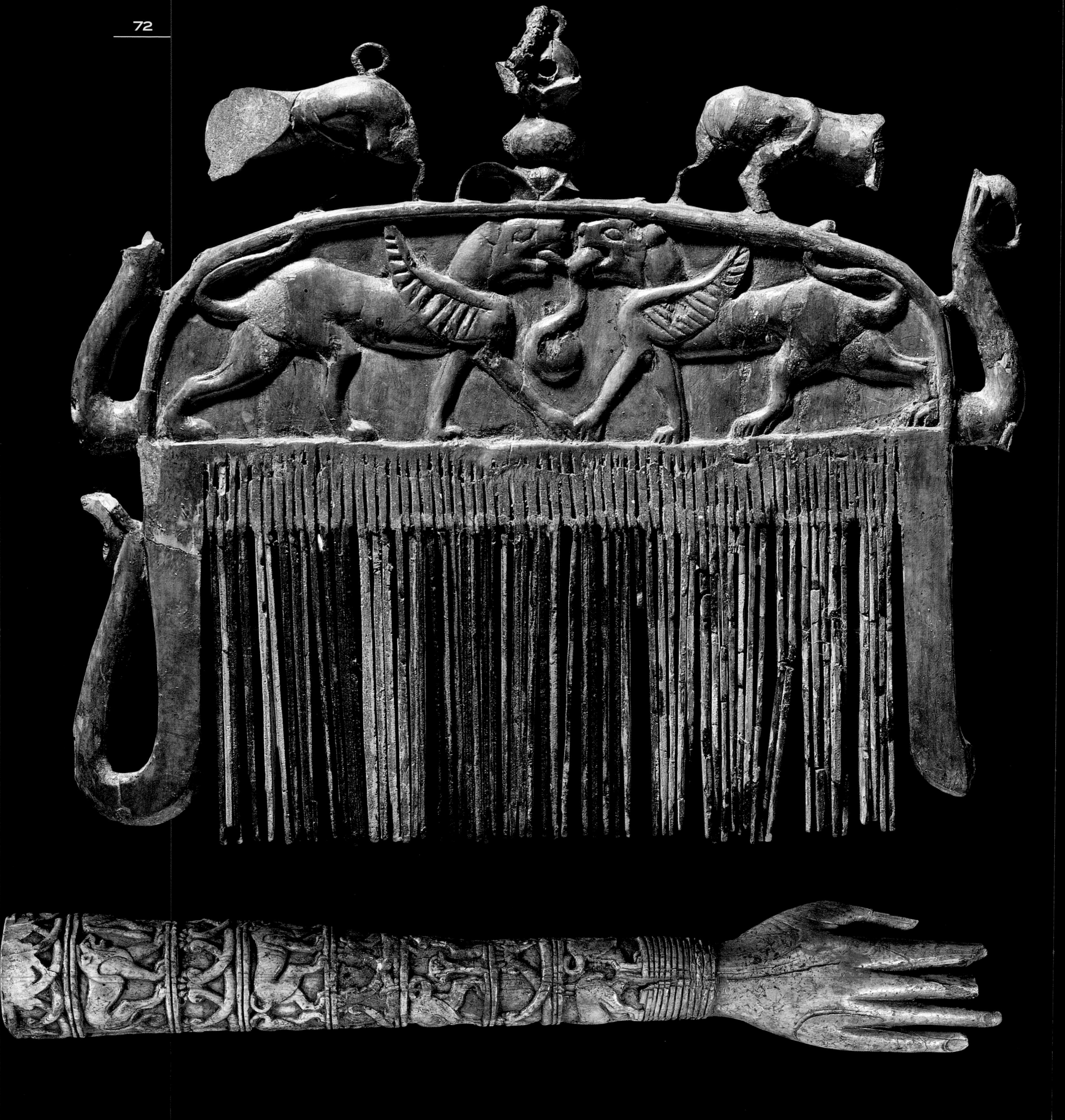

72 top - The ivory comb with relief decorations was found in a circle grave known as the Tomb of the Ivories at Marsiliana d'Albegna (Archaeological Museum, Florence).

72 bottom - The flabellum handle is richly decorated with overlaid bands bearing carved figures of mythical and real animals, and plant motifs. It is from the Barberini Tomb at Palestrina (Villa Giulia National Etruscan Museum, Rome).

73 left - This ivory vessel (pyx) is decorated on four registers with episodes from the *Odyssey*. This object was part of the furnishings from a female burial known as the Pania Tomb at Chiusi (Archaeological Museum, Florence).

73 right - The ivory pyx (late 7th century BC) is decorated with two bands depicting both mythical and real animals, as well as plant elements (Louvre Museum, Paris).

74 LEFT - THE URN MADE TO HOLD THE ASHES OF THE DEAD IS COMPOSED OF A BICONICAL IMPASTO VASE AND A LID DECORATED WITH A LIVELY BANQUET SCENE. IT IS FROM A TOMB AT MONTESCUDAIO AND DATES TO THE MID-7TH CENTURY BC (ARCHAEOLOGICAL MUSEUM, FLORENCE).

74 RIGHT - THE FOUR-WHEEL BRONZE AND WOODEN CHARIOT (RECONSTRUCTED IN MODERN TIMES) WAS USED TO TRANSPORT THE DEAD AND HOLDS A SIX-FOOTED BRONZE FUNERAL BED. IT IS FROM THE REGOLINI-GALASSI TOMB AT CERVETERI (VATICAN MUSEUMS, VATICAN CITY).

75 - THE CORRIDOR WITH A PSEUDO-OGIVAL ROOF AT THE REGOLINI-GALASSI TOMB REFLECTS THE MONUMENTALITY OF THE PRINCELY ETRUSCAN TOMBS OF THE MID-7TH CENTURY BC.

Nevertheless, the significance of these tombs does not lie only in the worth of the materials and the extraordinary richness of some of the objects found in them. Since the tomb was not merely a collection of seemingly unrelated objects but a refined symbolic construction, uniting objects that bore different messages, its importance must be sought in all the different elements of the furnishings, the presence of certain extremely significant objects and the specific way in which they were deposited. Analyzing all these elements is the only way we can understand such a complex ritual and shed light on the mental processes of the society that produced it.

There are many extraordinary examples, such as the ceremonial complexity of the burials in the Regolini-Galassi Tomb. This tomb is famous not only for its exceptional gold furnishings, but also the objects and accoutrements that exemplify all the phases of the funeral ritual, starting with the transport of the deceased on a four-wheel carriage. The one from the princely burial of the Monte Michele necropolis (Veii) is the only other example found in the Tyrrhenian area. The gold jewelry from the Tomb of the Lictor in Vetulonia is equally famous, and has yielded brooches and fibulae exquisitely decorated using the *pulviscolo* technique, providing an excellent idea of the skill of Etruscan goldsmiths. However, the tomb has also yielded a highly symbolic object, namely the bundle of rods bound around a two-edged axe with which the high-ranking figure was buried to symbolize his power.

The princely tombs also had lavish banquet services with tableware for wine, drinking sets, and equipment for cooking and carving meat. The central role of all these practices in aristocratic Etruscan societies is widely known. An evocative banquet scene created by a set of figurines in the round from the lid of an ossuary discovered at Montescudaio, near modern Volterra, sketches a vivid picture of this complex ritual.

76-77 - THIS PICTURE SHOWS THE INTERIOR OF THE TOMB OF THE FUNERAL BEDS (6TH CENTURY BC) DISCOVERED AT THE BANDITACCIA NECROPOLIS AT MODERN-DAY CERVETERI. THE SPACES, ARCHITECTURAL ELEMENTS, AND FUNERAL BEDS ARE CARVED FROM ROCK AND RESEMBLE THE ROOMS IN A HOME.

Pomp and power were celebrated through tombs, and the exceptional furnishings found in princely burials amply demonstrate this. However, the aristocratic élite did not show off their power through the display of luxury items alone. It was above all the type of tomb – the tumulus – that represented the highest expression of the aristocracy. Tumuli, which can be considered the prime manifestation of Etruscan funerary architecture, varied widely depending on the area and the period. The chambers could be fully or partially excavated into rock or built above the ground. The layout included various rooms whose interiors were carefully carved, faithfully imitating the structural elements and furnishings present in contemporary aristocratic residences. On the surface there was a cylindrical base (a drum) with a corridor (dromos) extending from it. The dromos often had

77 LEFT - THIS FASCINATING PICTURE OF THE BANDITACCIA NECROPOLIS SHOWS TUMULI OWNED BY MEMBERS OF THE CAERETAN ARISTOCRACY.

steps leading to the burial chamber, which was closed off by large stone blocks. Rising over the entire structure was the earthen tumulus with a hemispherical dome that became increasingly monumental over time. Next to it there was a type of podium that was used for religious purposes, and possibly also to observe the funeral games staged to honor the dead. The tumulus could hold several chamber tombs excavated at different levels and in different periods for members of the same family, constituting a formidable instrument for perpetuating its memory and continuity. Some of the giant tumuli at the necropolises, especially the one at Cerveteri, reached diameters of 165 ft (50 m) during the mid-7th century. These tumuli evidently served the purpose of self-celebration, and their sheer size emphasized their importance and the fact that they belonged to a certain family. The isolated tumuli in these areas served the same purpose, but also indicated ownership of the land.

77 RIGHT - THIS PICTURE SHOWS THE INTERIOR OF THE TUMULUS OF THE PAINTED ANIMALS, SO CALLED BECAUSE OF THE FRAGMENTARY FIGURES OF ANIMALS THAT DECORATED THE VESTIBULE. A LION WAS PAINTED NEAR THE FUNERAL BED (BANDITACCIA NECROPOLIS).

Several extraordinary examples of funerary architecture also document another interesting aspect of the Etruscan culture of the Orientalizing period: ancestor worship.

At Ceri, located in the territory of Cerveteri, the Tomb of the Statues has an atrium with two sculpted figures seated on semicircular thrones. In the Pietrera tumulus in Vetulonia, four pairs of standing figures were aligned along the entrance corridor, and five terracotta statuettes of seated male and female figures were found in the Tomb of the Five Chairs at Cerveteri. Given the fact that they were originally set on five chairs carved in tufa next to two semicircular thrones and an altar, the room in which the seats were carved for the statuettes may have been a small votive chapel.

The stone statues from Ceri and Vetulonia, which also bear witness to the appearance of monumental stone sculpture in Etruria, and the terracotta statuettes from Cerveteri are the images of ancestors evoked by patrician clans during their ritual ceremonies. Furthermore, based on their location in rooms next to the entrances to the respective tombs, they seem to indicate that the entrances to aristocratic residences had small votive chapels in which ancestors were honored. As we know, this custom was widespread among the Romans, who placed images of the *maiores* in the atrium.

78 - THIS PICTURE SHOWS THE BACK WALL OF ONE OF THE ROOMS IN THE TOMB OF THE FIVE CHAIRS AT CERVETERI. IN THE TOMB, FIVE TERRACOTTA STATUES OF MEN AND WOMEN, REPRESENTING THE FAMILY'S ANCESTORS, WERE SET ON FIVE CHAIRS CARVED FROM VOLCANIC TUFA. THE TOMB DATES TO THE

79 - THE SEATED MALE TERRACOTTA FIGURE IS FROM THE TOMB OF THE FIVE CHAIRS AT CERVETERI. THIS HIGH-RANKING FIGURE IS WEARING A TUNIC WITH A CHECKED DESIGN AND A RED MANTLE FASTENED ON THE SHOULDER BY A FIBULA. IT PROBABLY REPRESENTED ONE OF THE ANCESTORS OF THE DECEASED (CAPITOLINE

The large bearded male figures, wearing wide-brimmed hats that were undoubtedly a distinctive sign of princes, had their arms outstretched and clenched an attribute, perhaps a two-edged axe or a *lituus* (a crozier-like religious cult instrument). The female statues, which were smaller, wore full-length garments decorated along the hem. This is an impressive allegorical presentation of an otherworldly space in which the male and female figures can be identified as the images of ancestors intended to glorify the prince and protect his palace and its residents. They look down into the courtyard and observe the rituals of patri-

cian power that have been captured in the friezes of the decorative slabs. A long frieze extended around the portico, repeating four scenes: the assembly of the gods, the banquet scene, the wedding procession and a race of young men on horseback. All of these scenes celebrated the key moments of aristocratic ceremony and the lifestyle of patrician families. The monumental complex of Zone F at Acquarossa, datable to the first quarter of the 6th century BC, is another exceptional example of an aristocratic dwelling. Although it shares many of the same elements found at the palace at Murlo, it also has several unique features,

starting with the fact that it is part of an urban structure. The lay out is tripartite, but with an L-shaped portico and a small temple outside the palace. The latter element marks a clear-cut departure from Murlo, where sacred rituals were performed inside the palace. The fact that the temple structure was separate from the palace indicates that the prince of Acquarossa had lost certain privileges, such as those involving sacred rituals, which were probably conducted by others. The architectural decoration — above all the figured friezes of finishing slabs — clearly documents the new aristocratic ideology that predominated in the palace,

depicting themes that were very widespread in Etruria at the time: a banquet associated with a Dionysian dance, a procession of hoplites, horsemen and warriors climbing onto a chariot and, within this military parade, two of Heracles' labors, namely his battles with the Nemean lion and the Cretan bull. In the Acquarossa slabs, Murlo's model of aristocratic ceremony is replaced by the paradigm of tyrannical power, in which Heracles, who represented a specific ideological value, was the hero adopted by the Etruscan aristocracy as a model of behavior for those who conquered power through their own efforts.

The houses and palaces held another legacy of the aristocratic class that was at least as important as their precious objects and highly significant as an instrument to glorify the prince's role and prestige: writing.

The Etruscans had already adopted writing by the late 8th century BC, when they began to represent the sounds of their language using a Western Greek type of alphabetic writing that circulated in Etruria thanks to the establishment of Euboean colonies at Pithekoussai and Cumae. The presence of a Euboean-type letter "A," carved on several impasto spools from Veii, demonstrates its circulation. Use of the written word was thus one of the cultural innovations acquired through the Etruscans' encounter with the Greek world.

The Etruscan élites must have adopted this new instrument for several reasons, starting with their participation in increasingly complex and dynamic exchanges that required adequate means of communication. However, epigraphic documentation from the early 7th century BC demonstrates that writing was not used by the aristocracy for utilitarian purposes, but as a sign of their status and as an inherently prestigious activity on a social level.

Aristocrats used writing for formulaic terms that recalled completed exchanges or the name of the object's owner, as a way to "enrich" the items that circulated through ceremonial gift-giving, thereby sealing the relationships between princes. Moreover, the presence of impressed or painted inscriptions before firing pottery, evidently made by artisans, and the large number of seventh-century Etruscan inscriptions – much greater than those from coeval Greek cities – underscores how widespread the knowledge of writing must have been even outside restricted aristocratic circles.

Another very interesting aspect that can be gleaned from epigraphic documentation and that confirms the importance of writing and its role as a distinctive sign of the prince lies in the rise of the *nomen gentilicium* during this period. In inscriptions, the name of the giver or owner of the object was written with two terms, one of which, the *nomen gentilicium*, expressed appurtenance to a *gens* (hence the term *gentilicium*) or family, using a two-name system that is reflected even today by the custom of a first name and a surname. The introduction of the family name thus went hand in hand with the rise of the aristocratic élites, who underscored their status not only through burials in tumuli and precious furnishings, but also by indicating their descent.

Here as well, aristocratic burials have yielded another fundamental element: a series of unique objects, referred to as abecedaria, that have shed light on how people learned to write. They were educational instruments that served as reminders for those who used them. The ivory tablet from the Tomb of the Ivories at Marsiliana D'Albegna is a good example of an abecedarium; deposited with styluses, it had the alphabetic sequence engraved along the edge. There is also the so-called inkwell from Cerveteri, found in the area of the Regolini Galassi Tomb, which was a full-fledged spelling book.

84-85 - THIS BUCCHERO DRINKING VESSEL (*KANTHAROS*) BEARS AN INSCRIPTION, WRITTEN FROM RIGHT TO LEFT, READING "I BELONG TO," WHICH DOCUMENTS THE EXTENT OF WRITING IN ETRURIA BY THE END OF THE 7TH CENTURY BC (BRITISH MUSEUM, LONDON).

85 LEFT - THE GENTILITIAL NAME MEZENTIUS, LIKE THAT OF A CHARACTER FROM THE *AENEID*, IS INCISED ON THIS CUP (LOUVRE MUSEUM, PARIS).

85 RIGHT - THE BUCCHERO INKWELL FROM CERVETERI HAS A PRIMER AND AN ABECEDARIUM CARVED ON IT (VATICAN MUSEUMS, VATICAN CITY).

During this period, relations among the various Etruscan centers must have been quite lively, as demonstrated by findings from Cerveteri. The city's goods were brought not only to the princes of Vetulonia, who controlled mining resources, but also to the south – Latium – where aristocracies such as those of Palestrina oversaw trading that took place along the routes leading to the interior of the peninsula. It is logical to presume that relations were established by sea, along a route that covered the entire coast from Tuscany to Latium, subsequently moving inland along rivers.

The picture sketched out so far necessarily assumes the existence of infrastructures connected via navigation and vessels that were more evolved than the ones we have illustrated here. A pair of *oinochoai* (pitchers) made in Tarquinia and datable to the early 7th century BC depicts well-outfitted vessels organized into two fleets, respectively composed of five and six ships, with their sails unfurled. The hulls are rounded, and the ships have a pointed prow, a stern that curves inward and a tiller. Some of them have a ram at the end of the prow and a railing on the stern. Thus, it was a more complex type of boat that can also be seen on a "heron" plate made in Cerveteri and dating from the mid-7th century BC, which was found at a site in the Latium region, near Rome.

Of all the representations of ships, the one depicted on the Aristonothos krater is unquestionably the most important. This extremely important object was discovered in tomb in Cerveteri and dates back to the second half of the 7th century BC.

The krater is richly decorated with two very intricate scenes: one side depicts the well-known episode, recounted in the *Odyssey*, of the blinding of Polyphemus, and the other side depicts a naval battle. On the left there is a flat-hulled warship, handled by oarsmen and with four armed warriors, and the right side portrays a merchant ship with a deeper curved hull, fitted with a sail and with four armed men aboard.

The naval battle has been interpreted in various ways. Nevertheless, it seems to depict a clash between Etruscans and Greeks, as recounted in the passage from Strabo mentioned here, describing conflicts between these two populations before and during the colonization of western Sicily. At the same time, the fact that objects produced in Cerveteri have been found in Sicilian settings may indicate routes followed by Etruscan vessels that, in their travels, must have crossed paths with the Greeks who were in search of trade and places in which to settle.

The importance that the Etruscan aristocrats attributed to navigation is also confirmed by the representation of a ship that the wealthy owner of a tomb in Cerveteri, dating back to the mid-7th century BC, had painted behind his funeral bed to commemorate his seafaring activities. Unfortunately, this painting no longer exists. Life in the large proto-urban centers of the 7th century BC thus seems to have revolved around maritime activities, with well-outfitted masted ships, established routes and coasting trade organized with landing places along the shore.

Nevertheless, true ports with appropriate structures and large sanctuaries were not established until the 6th century BC, when urban forms became fully entrenched and navigation, sea routes and trade became the mainstays of Etruscan economic life.

88-89 - THIS RED-FIGURE IMPASTO OLLA, USED TO HOLD LIQUIDS, DEPICTS A SHIP WITH THREE OARSMEN. THE PROW IS SHAPED LIKE A BIRD AND THERE IS A STAG IN THE BACKGROUND. THE VASE WAS PART OF THE RICH FURNISHINGS FROM A TOMB IN BISENZIO AND WAS MADE IN THE LATE 8TH CENTURY BC (VILLA GIULIA NATIONAL ETRUSCAN MUSEUM, ROME).

89 - THE ARISTONOTHOS KRATER IS A MASTERPIECE OF VASE PAINTING. IT IS THE WORK OF A GREEK ARTISAN WHO WAS ACTIVE IN CERVETERI IN THE MID-7TH CENTURY BC. TWO SHIPS ARE DEPICTED ON THIS SIDE OF THE VASE. ONE IS A CARGO SHIP WITH A CURVED HULL, WHEREAS THE OTHER ONE – A WARSHIP WITH A RAM – IS MANNED BY OARSMEN AND IS ENGAGED IN A BATTLE AT SEA (CAPITOLINE MUSEUMS, ROME).

THE AGE OF EXPANSION:
THE URBAN CIVILIZATION

Political and Ideological Forms:
Cities and Necropolises
page 92

Temples and Religion
page 106

Seafaring and Trade
page 126

Marketplaces: Ports and Emporiums
page 128

Production: Resources and Crafts
page 132

Aristocrats and the Wealthy:
Life and Death
page 144

POLITICAL AND IDEOLOGICAL FORMS: CITIES AND NECROPOLISES

The radical process of organizing communities and settlements, which began in the 9th century BC with the formation of large proto-urban centers and continued with the affirmation of powerful aristocratic groups that controlled their resources and wealth, came to an end towards the beginning of the 6th century BC with the emergence of urban forms modeled after the Greek polis.

With the transition from proto-urban centers to cities, the economic and social organization of the Orientalizing period was abandoned. Major political changes occurred, as a result of which the power of the princes, founded on family ties and authority over the community, was curbed and replaced by a new order, based on more balanced distribution of wealth and the organization of the social structure into guilds.

This new order was imposed by a part of society composed of free individuals, a class of well-to-do people whose strength lay in production, trade and land ownership. All of these elements stemmed from a very favorable economic situation that arose at the beginning of the 6th century BC, but was rooted in the rapid rise in overproduction observed in the 7th century BC. This class of prosperous Etruscans — a different group with respect to the aristocrats, although they tried to imitate the lifestyle of the latter — was composed of members of gentilitial families, as is evident from

91 - THIS TERRACOTTA HEAD OF THE GOD HERMES WAS PART OF THE DECORATION ON THE SANCTUARY OF PORTONACCIO AT VEII (VILLA GIULIA NATIONAL ETRUSCAN MUSEUM, ROME).

92-93 - THIS PRECIOUS WREATH FROM THE 4TH CENTURY BC IS THE TYPE TRADITIONALLY PLACED IN THE BURIALS OF HIGH-RANKING FIGURES. IT IS COMPOSED OF A THIN GOLD BAND WITH LEAVES LAYERED OVER IT; SMALLER LEAVES SURROUND THE BULLA IN THE MIDDLE (KUNSTHISTORISCHES MUSEUM, VIENNA).

93 - THESE FRAGMENTS ARE FROM TERRACOTTA SHARDS USED TO DECORATE BUILDINGS. THEY WERE FOUND IN ROME AND VELLETRI (ANCIENT VELITRAE), AND DATE TO THE 6TH CENTURY BC (PALATINE ANTIQUARIUM / FORUM ANTIQUARIUM, ROME).

the two-name form they used. It was the city that best distinguished the Etruscans from the other populations of pre-Roman Italy. This is demonstrated by the fact that the ancients described them as "the builders of cities." The very name *Rasenna*, by which the Etruscans referred to themselves, means "part of the city." In other words, they considered themselves members of individual city-states, such as Veii, Tarquinia and Cerveteri.

We must turn to ancient sources to study the structure and sociopolitical organization of the city, about which little is known due to the lack of a direct tradition. Many sources tell us that the cities were headed by a king, using the term *lucu-*

mo to refer to this figure. This word probably indicated the Etruscan kings of the Archaic period, and this role must have merged supreme judiciary power with the position of head of the army and religious leader. The sources also tell us about some of the exterior attributes of the monarchy and the ceremonies considered specifically Etruscan in origin, which were later adopted by the Romans: the gold crown of oak leaves, the ivory scepter, the ivory *sella curulis*, the gold bulla, the bundle of rods bound around a two-edged axe, and other symbols of power such as the *toga palmata*, the *tunica picta* or embroidered toga, the *toga praetexta*, which had a purple border, and the triumph ceremony.

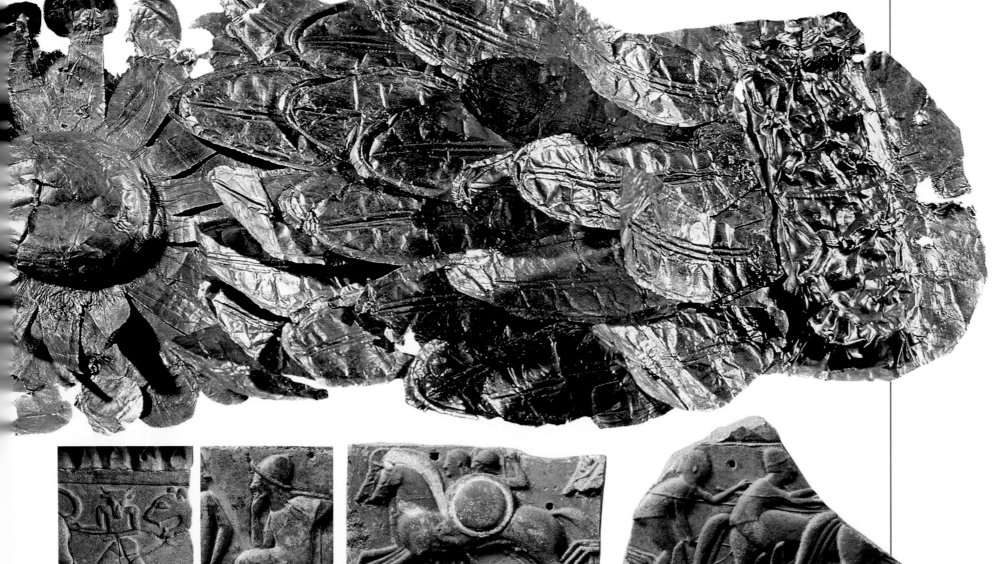

The religious monarchy was flanked by personal power that was "tyrannical" in nature. Reformers successfully consolidated city power against the particularism of individual aristocratic groups by creating political and religious institutions that expressed cohesion and a community identity. In large cities, this led to the planning of public spaces that became the privilege of a larger part of the community. The city was thus laid out with public and sacred monuments, artisan districts and marketplaces, and it also staged political and religious festivals and ceremonies.

The writers of antiquity provide fascinating accounts of the deeds of the last three kings of Rome, Tarquinius Priscus (Tarquin the Elder), Servius Tullius and Tarquinius Superbus (Tarquin the Proud), all of whom were of Etruscan descent, painting a vivid picture of the organization and urban transformation of the Etruscan cities.

According to the sources, Tarquinius Priscus, who ruled from last decade of the 7th century BC until the early 6th century, oversaw extensive public works, such as draining the marshes to create a site for the Forum, erecting pub-

lic buildings such as the Curia (Hostilia) and the Regia, constructing the *cloacae* (sewers), particularly the Cloaca Maxima, and doing work on the Capitoline Hill in order to build the Temple of Jupiter Capitoline. Another very significant aspect discussed by the ancients is the role that the first of the Tarquins played in launching institutional reforms and introducing Etruscan habits and customs to Rome, such as the use of royal insignias, the triumph ceremony and games, all of which would later become Roman traditions.

With regard to Servius Tullius, who ruled in the mid-6th century BC, the sources focus in particular on his work to reform the army through the century structure; his legislative reforms with the classification of citizens based on their economic level – the census – and the creation of four urban tribes; and the introduction of the *aes signatum*, an early form of coinage. He also gave Rome a new layout by building two large sanctuaries and the great wall around the city. Servius Tullius' work as a reformer has been credited with promoting the middle classes rather than the

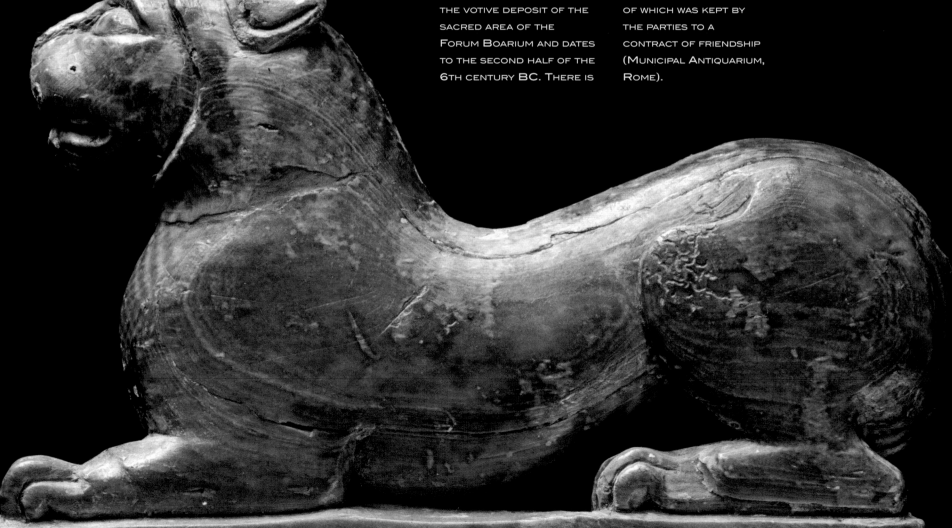

members of the ancient aristocracy. The sources recall Tarquinius Superbus – the last king of Rome, who ruled until the end of the 6th century – as a tyrant, and his name reflects this. Unlike his predecessor, Tarquinius Superbus seems to have concentrated exclusively on large-scale works, notably the great tutelary temple on the Capitoline Hill dedicated to Jupiter.

Although this information is vague and its attribution is unclear in some cases, it nevertheless contains a kernel of historical truth that is essential for reconstructing the Etruscan world of the 6th century BC.

The coexistence of various important centers that were organized and distinguished by their own powers, characteristics and customs seems to have been inspired by the city-states of the coeval western Greek colonies. This political structure was referred to in Latin as *populus*, which indicated the residents of the city, i.e., the citizens of Veii, Tarquinia, Vulci and so on. Consequently, it underscored the autonomy and political particularism typical of the Etruscan world, in which each city-state was politically and culturally independent in its internal administration, trade, maritime traffic, foreign policy and even craftsmanship.

The formation of the city-state led the creation of a type of "association" that the ancient sources referred to as "the twelve peoples" (*duodecim populi*) or Dodecapolis. The term referred to a federal system composed of the twelve most important cities of Etruria proper, which were paralleled by 12 cities in Northern and Southern Etruria, creating a "national" identification reminiscent of the twelve cities of the Ionian League.

As noted in the sources, this confederation was a political institution with a common site, the sanctuary of Voltumna (*Fanum Voltumnae*) near Orvieto (Volsinii), where solemn festivals and games, celebrated annually, were attended by the representatives of the individual cities. Although these events were prevalently religious, as the title of *sacerdos*, used to designate the elective head of the league, seems to suggest, decisions were also made, including political resolutions to undertake military actions or form alliances.

95 TOP - THIS BRONZE INGOT BEARS A DESIGN REFERRED TO AS "WITHERED BRANCH." SUCH BARS WERE MADE TO MEET TRADE NEEDS THAT AROSE STARTING IN THE MID-6TH CENTURY BC (BRITISH MUSEUM, LONDON).

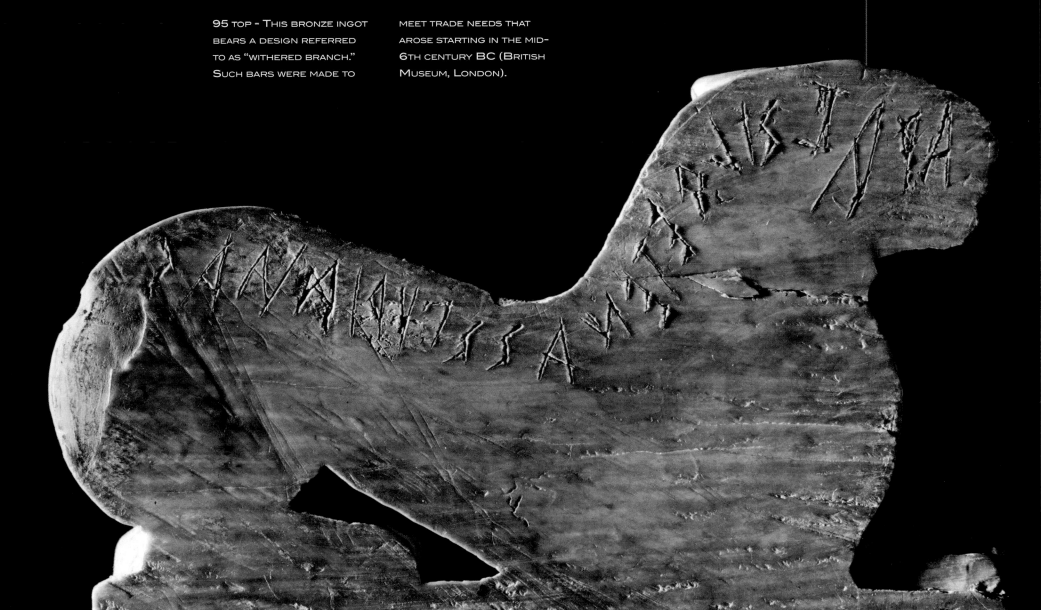

96 - This antefix (an architectural element that was mounted on the ends of roof beams) portrays a Gorgon's head with a rich painted decoration. It is from Capua, an important Etruscan city in Campania, and dates to the 6th century BC (Campano Museum, Santa Maria Capua Vetere).

97 left - The bronze lebes, whose lid is decorated with figures on horseback around a satyr and a maenad, was a cinerary urn. Found in a tomb in Capua, it was made between the late 6th and early 5th centuries BC (British Museum, London).

97 right - The bronze krater, from the tomb of a high-ranking woman at the Capua necropolis, has richly decorated scroll handles. Made in Laconia, it dates to the first half of the 6th century BC (Archaeological Museum, Capua).

The leaders attributed with establishing the league of the twelve peoples promoted the widespread colonization of two areas – Campania and the Po area – in which the Etruscan presence dated back to very ancient times.

This enormous expansion led Livy, the Roman historian who lived during the Augustan Age, to comment, "Before the Roman supremacy, the power of the Tuscans [Etruscans] was widely extended both by sea and land." He also cited the etymology of the names of the Tyrrhenian and Adriatic Seas: the former from the name the Greeks attributed to the Etruscans, and the latter from the city of Adria, which was considered an Etruscan city.

In his *Naturalis Historia*, Pliny the Elder, who lived in the 1st century AD, discussed the territories outside Etruria proper but under its domination, noting that the region from Sorrento to the Sele River was once in the hands of the Etruscans. This is echoed by other writers, who refer to an Etruscan dodecapolis in Campania, headed by Capua.

These centers can be discerned in a series of settlements discovered in Campania. Several landing places that served as "commercial ports" and bases for expansion into the lower Tyrrhenian have been pinpointed along the coast. Moreover,

several settlements were founded in the heart the Campanian plains to undertake intensive farming in an area famed for its productiveness.

The plains of the Po River were also colonized extensively as part of the Etruscans' search for arable land and commercial outlets. The cities of Marzabotto and Spina were founded as a result, one located in the river valley of the Reno along a route that was fundamental for trade, and the other near a large lagoon with a canal connecting it to the. At the same time, Felsina (Roman Bononia and modern-day Bologna) was completely reorganized: an important center for crafts and the distribution of goods, it was also famed for its intensively exploited agricultural resources. Thus, the Po valley seems to have been a well-organized territory in which, according to the sources, the various cities had formed a political and religious league similar to that of Etruria proper.

The ancient sources discussing Rome's Etruscan kings describe an urban layout with colossal constructions, city walls, sewer systems and various public and sacred foundations, which must certainly have been used in coeval Etruscan cities. So far, however, there is little documentation confirming this.

Veii is an excellent example of the large cities of Southern Etruria. In the mid-6th century BC significant urban planning was undertaken on the plateau of Piazza d'Armi, with a main avenue that was about 16 ft (4.8 m) wide and was intersected by smaller roads that were about 10 ft (3 m) wide, a square with a large open cistern and the earliest city walls. It seems that additional building work was done on the plateau at the end of the 6th century BC, as indicated by monumentalization of the road. This work can be linked with the construction of a gate, porticoes and workshops.

Important urban transformations were also carried out in Cerveteri between the 6th and 5th centuries BC, with houses, cisterns, and an oval construction that was least 115 ft (35 m) in diameter and was used for assemblies and other events.

The signs of growing public intervention in city planning can clearly be seen in the permanent settlements established on the coast, such as Pyrgi, which seems to have been founded with an essentially octagonal layout and an enormous straight road stretching for approximately 7.5 miles (12 km) to Cerveteri. Such intervention is also evident in mining areas,

such as the settlement discovered near Lake Accesa, in the backlands of Vetulonia, where the signs of a uniform layout have been found. The settlement was divided into several nuclei with about 10 relatively standardized dwellings, each of which had 2 or 3 rooms and a vestibule; there seems to be no marked social diversification.

Nevertheless, only in newly established cities such as Marzabotto and Spina do we find a redefined urban structure, and this is due to the formation and development of the middle class, which promoted egalitarian and standardizing trends. Thus, the Hippodamian model (named after Hippodamus of

100-101 - THIS AERIAL VIEW OF THE SITE OF VULCI SHOWS THE *DECUMANUS*, THE AREA OF THE GREAT TEMPLE (LEFT) AND THE URBAN SECTOR WITH THE HOUSE OF THE CRYPTOPORTICUS AND THE MITHRAEUM (RIGHT).

100 bottom - THE PICTURE SHOWS AN OLLA SET ON A STOVE. BOTH OF THESE IMPASTO ARTIFACTS ARE FROM THE HOUSE OF THE IMPLUVIUM AT ROSELLE AND DATE TO THE 7TH CENTURY BC (ARCHAEOLOGICAL MUSEUM, GROSSETO).

Miletus, an urban theorist who lived in the mid-5th century BC and designed several Greek cities), with roads intersecting at right angles and *insulae* ('islands') with uniform houses, proved to be ideal. At Spina, which was founded in the 6th century BC, the main area had an orthogonal layout and roads were essentially replaced by navigable canals, similar those of Venice. Marzabotto, which was built at the beginning of the 5th century BC, unquestionably provides the clearest example of the Hippodamian model. It was divided into 8 main districts, each composed of 5 *insulae* with 7 or 8 very large courtyard houses, streets with shops, and fountains that assured the city's water supply.

The houses, with continuous stone walls, evoked a new model in which the rooms were set around an atrium, as seen in the House of the Impluvium at Roselle. This model would be the archetypal Roman *domus* (house) for centuries to come. These dwellings used ingenious solutions to collect rainwater and to provide lighting and ventilation. There were also several key innovations, such as small rooms that may have been used as bathrooms.

101 LEFT - THIS IS AN AERIAL VIEW OF VEII, WHICH UNDERWENT GREAT URBAN DEVELOPMENT IN THE 7TH CENTURY BC.

101 right - THIS IS A CLOSE-UP OF THE SETTLEMENT IN THE BORGO AREA OF SAN GIOVENALE. THE BUILDING FOUNDATIONS, MADE OF STONE BLOCKS, DATE TO THE 6TH CENTURY BC.

102 TOP - DADO TOMBS FROM THE 6TH CENTURY BC CAN BE SEEN AT THE BANDITACCIA NECROPOLIS OF CERVETERI.

102 BOTTOM - DADO TOMBS WERE ERECTED IN THE AREA OF THE CAERETAN NECROPOLIS NOW KNOWN AS VIA DEI MONTI DELLA TOLFA. THEY WERE BUILT ALONGSIDE TUMULI FROM THE ARCHAIC PERIOD (LEFT).

102-103 - THE FAÇADES OF A SERIES OF CLIFF TOMBS BENEATH THE WALLS OF CERVETERI IMITATE THE EXTERIOR OF A CIVIL STRUCTURE.

The relatively uniform scenario offered by private construction, with standards that can be defined as average, reflects widespread prosperity and the ideological move towards an egalitarian society during the Archaic period. This is also evident in the spatial organization of several funerary sites, such as the Banditaccia Necropolis (Cerveteri) and the Crocefisso del Tufo Necropolis (Orvieto).

At Cerveteri, a new type of tomb was introduced in place of the large tumuli. They are referred to as dado or cube tombs due to their shape, which saved a great deal of space and facilitated planning, as the tombs could be positioned along straight roads or around open spaces with a regular perimeter.

The most intensive and systematic application of this type of necropolis can be found in Orvieto (ancient Volsinii), where the tombs – all of which cube-shaped – were made entirely of blocks and laid out on parallel terraces. The lintels of the façades, which were identical, bore the name of the owner of the tomb. This indicates that Orvieto had approximately 100 middle-class *nomina gentilicia*, reflecting the egalitarian trend of Etruscan society. In essence, between the 6th and 5th centuries BC Etruria was a complex political and economic entity that played an important role in the Mediterranean scenario. However, the international situation changed in 480 BC with the Greeks' victory at Salamis and the Carthaginians' defeat at Himera at the hands of the Syracusans. After overpowering Carthage, Hiero of Syracuse turned against the Etruscans, who suffered a serious naval defeat at Cumae in 474. Syracuse thus gained control over the traffic of the Tyrrhenian Sea at the same time as Athens, which focused its expansionist aims on the West. The terrible defeat at Cumae mainly affected the southern maritime cities, whose economy was based on trade. As a result, private demand declined in this area during the 5th century BC, leading to a decrease in public investments.

The economic hub shifted to the inland and Po areas, which continued to prosper to a certain extent thanks to agricultural resources and trade routes to the north.

104-105 - THESE TWO PAINTED TERRACOTTA PLAQUES (FIRST HALF OF THE 6TH CENTURY BC), DEPICTING ELEGANTLY GARBED MEN AND WOMEN IN A RITUAL SCENE, DECORATED THE WALLS OF A CHAMBER TOMB AT THE BANDITACCIA NECROPOLIS IN CERVETERI (BRITISH MUSEUM, LONDON).

TEMPLES AND RELIGION

The rise of urban forms led to a change in the organization of sacred areas, which were no longer the privilege of aristocrats. As a result, they were not situated inside their homes, instead requiring structures designed for the religious sphere and built in public areas.

An "architectural category" thus arose for the temple, the "house" of the deities. This type of architecture was very distinctive and had specific monumental forms. It also required rich terracotta ornamentation that, by highlighting its sacredness, made the structure instantly recognizable.

The Etruscans chose a type of building with a three-room plan that had already been adopted for dwellings and tombs, in place of the single-room or *oikos* temples of the previous period. The result was a typically Etruscan invention: the triple-cella temple with a front entrance, embellished by a double row of columns and set on a tall base with steps on the short side. The ancient writers – Vitruvius in particular – referred to this type as "Tuscan," an adjective that evidently

referred to the fact that it was Etruscan. As opposed to Greek temples, this type was set on a high podium, a feature connected with distinctive Etruscans religious and augural practices through which the space for the deity was consecrated, delimited and defined as a *templum*, which meant "space marked out." The elevated portion, which was thus "marked out" with respect to its surroundings and easy to recognize, was a specific religious device that acquired architectural value, and it was a feature found only in the religious architecture of ancient Italy.

The temple was then embellished and distinguished by an intricate terracotta decorative system that displayed images of the gods and theirs sagas to the faithful. These works drew on the extraordinary legacy of figurations taken from Greek mythology and epics, which gradually penetrated the Etruscan mentality and came to distinguish all the architectural ornamentation of temples starting in the second half of the 7th century BC.

106 - THE PICTURE SHOWS THE MODEL OF A TERRACOTTA TEMPLE WITH FLUTED COLUMNS, FIGURES ON THE PEDIMENT, AND TWO PALMETTE ANTEFIXES ON THE SIDES. IT IS FROM VULCI AND DATES TO THE LATE 3RD CENTURY BC (VILLA GIULIA NATIONAL ETRUSCAN MUSEUM, ROME).

107 TOP - THE PAINTED TERRACOTTA ANTEFIX PORTRAYS THE HEAD OF A MAENAD WITH A NIMBUS DECORATED WITH PLANT MOTIFS. IT DATES TO THE 5TH CENTURY BC (ARCHAEOLOGICAL MUSEUM, ORVIETO).

107 BOTTOM - THE PAINTED TERRACOTTA ANTEFIX PORTRAYS A SILENUS HEAD WITH A NIMBUS DECORATED WITH PLANT MOTIFS. IT DATES TO THE 5TH CENTURY BC (ARCHAEOLOGICAL MUSEUM, ORVIETO).

108 - THE TERRACOTTA HEAD
MAY HAVE BEEN PART OF THE
STATUE OF A YOUNG WARRIOR
THAT DECORATED THE
PEDIMENT OF THE BELVEDERE
TEMPLE AT ORVIETO (C. FAINA
MUSEUM, ORVIETO).

109 - THE BEARDED HEAD IS
FROM A STATUE THAT
DECORATED THE PEDIMENT OF
THE TEMPLE OF VIA SAN
LEONARDO, IN MODERN-DAY
ORVIETO, AND DATES TO THE
EARLY 4TH CENTURY BC (C.
FAINA MUSEUM, ORVIETO).

Building a temple was clearly very demanding work that required great organization. Various phases were involved in building the structure, such as digging the foundation pit, completing the earthworks, laying stone blocks for the foundation, executing the structural work and making the terracotta ornamentation, composed of large acroterial statues (set along the main roof beam), antefixes (elements set at the ends of the eave tiles) and slabs covering the pediment (arranged to cover the ends of the main roof beam). Moreover, construction called for complex operations that required a great deal of know-how and technical skill, ranging from the choosing the clay to making the impasto, modeling the parts to be molded, coloring and firing, which was especially difficult for large items. As a result, the individual parts had to be fired separately and then assembled and finished on site.

All of this led to the use of specialized workers who were distinguished not only by their specific manual skills but also by the great creativity that was required to satisfy the needs of public patrons who wanted increasingly ambitious projects. The workers probably set up a workshop near the temple for the duration of construction and then moved on to the next job. This would explain why temples in different areas had decorative slabs made with the same molds.

Sanctuaries were gradually being built in the cities. They were political and religious centers in which public power concentrated the greatest financial effort combined with a profound cultural and ideological commitment. In these structures, essential urban functions were conducted alongside strictly religious ones.

Urban sanctuaries were set up within the great metropolises. However, these cities were also encircled by a series of suburban sanctuaries close to the city walls, which permitted contact with the outside world; the Portonaccio sanctuary at Veii is a good example. Moreover, there were also sanctuaries far from the cities, built by ports and marketplaces. Referred to as extra-urban sanctuaries, they were situated at sites that were strategic for communications and international trade. They played an economic role as the headquarters of the authorities responsible for commercial transactions, but also as served as deposits for great riches. The most famous of these was Pyrgi, the port of Cerveteri.

110 LEFT - THIS ANTEFIX, DECORATED WITH AN INVERTED PALMETTE AND SCALLOPED NIMBUS, IS FROM THE TEMPLE OF MATER MATUTA AT SATRICUM AND DATES TO THE 5TH CENTURY BC (VILLA GIULIA NATIONAL ETRUSCAN MUSEUM, ROME).

110 RIGHT - THE ANTEFIX DECORATED WITH THE FACE OF A BEARDED GORGON AND SCALLOPED NIMBUS IS FROM THE TEMPLE OF MATER MATUTA AT SATRICUM AND DATES TO THE 5TH CENTURY BC (VILLA GIULIA NATIONAL ETRUSCAN MUSEUM, ROME).

111 - This painted terracotta element depicts a Gorgon mask, underscoring the figure's monstrous features (wild stare and prominent eyeteeth). It decorated the Belvedere Temple at Orvieto and dates to the 5th century BC (Archaeological Museum, Orvieto).

112 - THE HEAD OF A BALD AND
BEARDED OLD MAN IS FROM A STATUE
THAT DECORATED THE PEDIMENT ON THE
BACK OF THE BELVEDERE TEMPLE AT
ORVIETO. IT WAS MADE IN THE LATE 5TH
OR EARLY 4TH CENTURY BC (C. FAINA
MUSEUM, ORVIETO).

113 - THE LARGE PAINTED TERRACOTTA
ANTEFIX DEPICTS A SATYR AND A
MAENAD DANCING, AS THE LATTER
PLAYS THE CASTANETS. THIS ARTIFACT
DECORATED THE TEMPLE OF MATER
MATUTA AT SATRICUM (VILLA GIULIA
NATIONAL ETRUSCAN MUSEUM, ROME).

The suburban sanctuary of Portonaccio, which was consecrated to Minerva and other deities, went through various construction phases, each of which has yielded exceptional documentation, particularly concerning Archaic terracotta statuary.

A magnificent male torso from the mid-6th century BC has been linked with the first phase of the sanctuary. The torso was part of a large erect statue, and its careful craftsmanship seems to be the work of a Veiian artist named Volcanius. The sculptor was cited by the ancient sources not only for his skill, but also because Tarquinius Priscus summoned him to Rome. This episode is recounted by Pliny the Elder. "Volcanius was summoned from Veii, and entrusted by Tarquinius Priscus with making the figure of Jupiter, which he intended to consecrate in the Capitol; ... this Jupiter was made of clay, and ... hence arose the custom of painting it with minium ... [T]he Hercules was executed, which, even to this day, is named at Rome from the material of which it is composed. Such, in those times, were the most esteemed statues of the gods."

The sanctuary was restructured in the late 6th century and a temple was built. Because of its exquisite ornamentation, this temple can be considered the most important in Etruria. The building was ornately decorated with antefixes, slabs covering the pediment and more than 10 acroterial statues (life-sized or slightly larger), which represented the most original and intricate part of the entire complex.

The temple must have had a powerful impact on the faithful approaching the sanctuary because, viewed laterally and from a distance along the obligatory route next to the temple, the statues rising from the roof must have looked as if they were suspended in midair. Given that they were made in three sizes, they must have been divided into groups of two or three, and they represented different mythological episodes: Apollo and Hercules fighting over the Hind of Ceryneia; Leto holding little Apollo in her arms as she flees from the serpent Python; and the figures of Hermes, the monstrous Lernaean Hydra and a sphinx.

The sculptor who created the statues has been referred to as the Apollo Master, in relation to the most famous and emblematic figure of the entire decoration. The "expert in coroplastic art," who was never named by the ancient sources but was indicated as the sculptor of the four-horse chariot at the temple of Capitoline Jupiter in Rome, commissioned by Tarquinius Superbus, may have been a Veiian master.

These exceptional works showed a powerful Ionian influence and were executed in a style that paid close attention to elaborate draping and volume. The artist's skill is also underscored by his attention to modeling, which is evident in the seemingly exaggerated torsion of the bodies, clearly taking into account the fact that the statues would be viewed laterally and from below at a distance.

At the sanctuary of Portonaccio, important archaeological findings close to the votive chapel of Minerva include a beautiful terracotta group that is three-fourths life size. It depicts Hercules and Minerva as the goddess presents the hero to the gods at the end of his 12 labors. The group was probably displayed near this sacred place as an important offering to the goddess. The donor was undoubtedly a very prestigious figure, as indicated by the type of image he chose for his treasury: Hercules was the favorite hero of Archaic royalty, who identified with the hero whose deeds allowed him to rise to power.

114 - THE TERRACOTTA BUST WAS PART OF A STATUE OF A NUDE FIGURE — POSSIBLY HERACLES — WITH WELL-DEFINED PECTORALS AND A BEAUTIFULLY SCULPTED BODY. IT WAS PART OF THE DECORATION FROM A TEMPLE AT THE SANCTUARY OF PORTONACCIO AT VEII AND DATES TO THE MID-6TH CENTURY BC (VILLA GIULIA NATIONAL ETRUSCAN MUSEUM, ROME).

115 - THE TERRACOTTA STATUE (LEFT) PORTRAYS THE GODDESS LETO HOLDING LITTLE APOLLO IN HER ARMS. THE STATUE ON THE RIGHT DEPICTS HERACLES BRANDISHING HIS CLUB AND HOLDING A STAG BOUND BETWEEN HIS LEGS. THEY WERE PART OF THE ACROTERIAL DECORATION ON THE SANCTUARY OF PORTONACCIO AT VEII (VILLA GIULIA NATIONAL ETRUSCAN MUSEUM, ROME).

116 - This close-up of the head of the statue of Apollo, from Veii, shows the stylized detailing of the god's hair (Villa Giulia National Etruscan Museum, Rome).

117 - This is one of the masterpieces of Etruscan art in the Ionic style. It is a terracotta statue of Apollo that, with statues of other gods, decorated the central beam of the sanctuary of Portonaccio at Veii. The figure presents exceptional balance between body mass and the treatment of the surfaces the garments; it dates to the late 6th century BC (Villa Giulia National Etruscan Museum, Rome).

Unlike the suburban sanctuary of Portonaccio, which was not mentioned in literature, the extra-urban sanctuary of Pyrgi is one of the few cited by Greek and Roman sources. At the end of the 6th century BC, the city of Cerveteri undertook an ambitious building program near its port town. Over the course of 50 years, the work transformed the sanctuary of Pyrgi into the largest in Etruria, covering an area of 1.5 acres (0.4 hectares), or 5 times that of Portonaccio. Temple B was the first to be built in the sprawling sacred area near the shore. This large temple, built in the Greek rather than the Tuscan style, had columns on all four sides and was dedicated to Uni, the supreme goddess who was the lady of childbirth and light, and the protectress of seafaring. Several fascinating elements from the temple's terracotta decorations have been discovered, such as a series of hand-modeled antefixes. One of them is an intriguing Negroid head, distinguished by the figure's black face and tightly curled hair. A long building was erected next to Temple B. Composed of approximately 20 cellae, it housed the deity's priestesses. The building was probably decorated with a series of antefixes, whose types are not documented elsewhere, that were created specifically for the Pyrgi sanctuary. They were full-figure antefixes positioned on the long side of the building to create a powerful effect, and they represented unique images such as the horse-taming goddess, a winged demon with the head of a rooster, and a solar deity on a rosette.

However, the most extraordinary discovery involved three gold tablets that were placed near Temple B when the sanctuary was abandoned. They were carefully rolled up and still had the nails that were probably used to hang them on the wooden doors of the temple. Two of the plates have a bilingual inscription in Etruscan and Phoenician, in which Thefarie Velianas, king of Cerveteri, dedicated a "holy place" and a cult statue to a goddess, referred to as Astarte in Phoenician and Uni in Etruscan, for helping him rise to power. The third plate bears an Etruscan text without a corresponding Phoenician inscription, in which the king commemorated the founding of the cult and detailed its rituals. These inscriptions are extraordinary for several reasons. First of all, Thefarie Velianas, king of Cerveteri, is the only figure in Etruscan history who is known through a direct and contemporary source. Moreover, since the document was drawn up in two languages, it demonstrates ties between the Etruscans and the Carthaginians, about which there is extensive information in the ancient sources. It is possible that two languages were used due to the presence of foreign priestesses responsible for the cult of Uni/Astarte, and that they came from Eryx, a city situated in the area of Sicily controlled by the Carthaginians. Eryx was the site of a famous temple dedicated to the Mediterranean goddess of fertility: the Punic Astarte.

Nevertheless, scholars have also shown great interest in the gold tablets due to the fact that there are very few bilingual inscriptions with the Etruscan language. Therefore, the long inscription from Pyrgi is a exceptional resource that has added to our knowledge of this language, despite the fact that the correspondence between the two Etruscan and Phoenician texts strictly involves content and the translation is not literal.

In the second half of the 5th century the sacred precinct was doubled and Temple A was built. Like Temple B, it was

monumental in size, but this one was constructed in the Tuscan style, with three cellae and three rows of four columns along the front. It was unquestionably built by the city of Cerveteri as a way to affirm its maritime superiority following the Etruscans' heavy defeat by the Syracusans at Cumae in 474 BC. Because of Temple A's proximity to the sanctuary's main entrance, the back of the temple, which was clearly visible to visitors as they entered, was richly adorned. The pediment had three large terracotta slabs, and it has been possible to reassemble the middle one. It was decorated with a very complex high relief, with projecting bodies and heads rendered on multiple levels. A number of clever corrections were adopted so that the figuration could be appreciated viewed from below or afar.

The intricate decoration illustrates the episode of the Seven against Thebes, which was widely recounted in Etruria but was rarely represented in Greece, where the myth was considered the height of ungodliness. The figures portrayed on the slab at Pyrgi have been captured as they are being punished by the gods for their evil and sacrilegious behavior. Capaneus is struck by Zeus' thunderbolt and Tydeus shocks Athena, who was about to make him immortal, because she has seen him bite into Melanippus' open skull to eat his brains. This artifact is extremely important for studying the culture of Archaic Etruria, because it reveals the Etruscans' profound knowledge of Greek mythology and their ability to use it for their own ends. Indeed, Cerveteri's choice of this theme was not a random one. The episode of the Seven against Thebes and their sacrilegious deeds was employed as a way to accuse the Syracusans, who had pursued and then vanquished the Etruscans in battle, of impiety.

118 - THIS HIGH RELIEF DECORATED THE END OF THE MAIN BEAM OF TEMPLE A AT THE SANCTUARY AT PYRGI. IT ILLUSTRATES EPISODES FROM THE MYTH OF THE SEVEN AGAINST THEBES, DEPICTING CAPANEUS STRUCK BY ZEUS AND TYDEUS DEVOURING MELANIPPUS' BRAIN. THIS MASTERPIECE OF ETRUSCAN ART IS FROM THE FIRST HALF OF THE 5TH CENTURY BC (VILLA GIULIA NATIONAL ETRUSCAN MUSEUM, ROME).

119 - THIS GOLD PLATE, ALONG WITH TWO OTHERS, FORMED A TRIPTYCH WITH A BILINGUAL INSCRIPTION IN ETRUSCAN AND PUNIC CHARACTERS WITH A CAERETAN KING'S DEDICATION TO THE GODDESS UNI/ASTARTE AND A SHORTER ETRUSCAN INSCRIPTION DETAILING CULT RITUALS. THESE PRICELESS PLATES ARE FROM THE ENCLOSURE OF AREA C OF THE SANCTUARY AT PYRGI AND DATE TO THE 5TH CENTURY BC (VILLA GIULIA NATIONAL ETRUSCAN MUSEUM, ROME).

Many of Etruria's countless sacred sites are famous not for their extant buildings or elaborate ornamentation, but because of the votive material they have yielded, often in large quantities, expressing the religiosity of the Etruscan culture in all its phases.

These artifacts were the gifts of the faithful to the gods to express their gratitude or ask for help, and they were displayed inside the temples. Once the temples were full of votive offerings, since these objects could not be destroyed or sold – they were the god's property – they were buried in large pits. Concealed from view, these pits were gradually forgotten and long outlasted the buildings themselves. As a result, they have come down to our own day and age.

Although people would donate all kinds of things, they preferred to offer images of the deity venerated at the temple or of the worshipper making the offering. Religious implements and the images of sacrificial animals were also offered. In the case of deities of health, the worshipper would offer a terracotta reproduction of the diseased part of the body, asking the god to heal it or thanking the god for having done so.

The enormous numbers of gifts found at sanctuaries include some of the highest quality, such as the large terracotta groups discovered at Portonaccio. The bronze votive statue known as the Todi Mars, dating to the 5th century BC and commissioned from a workshop near Orvieto by a prestigious client, probably of Celtic origin, is from a later phase, as is the famous Chimera, the mythological monster with a lion's body and three heads, which was probably offered by a great prince at a suburban sanctuary near Arezzo (ancient Arretium) during the first half of the 4th century BC.

120 - THIS BEARDED HEAD WITH A CROWN IS FROM THE CAMPETTI VOTIVE DEPOSIT AT VEII. THE TERRACOTTA ARTIFACT WAS CRAFTED IN THE MID-5TH CENTURY BC (VILLA GIULIA NATIONAL ETRUSCAN MUSEUM, ROME).

121 - THIS BRONZE FIGURINE DEPICTS A YOUNG MAN PRAYING, HIS ARMS OPEN IN ADORATION AND A PATERA IN HIS RIGHT HAND. THE ARTIFACT IS FROM THE VOTIVE DEPOSIT OF MONTE ACUTO RAGAZZA (ARCHAEOLOGICAL MUSEUM, BOLOGNA).

122 LEFT – THIS BRONZE VOTIVE FIGURINE OF THE GODDESS MENERVA READY TO ATTACK DATES TO THE FIRST QUARTER OF THE 5TH CENTURY BC (ESTENSE MUSEUM, MODENA).

122 RIGHT – THIS BRONZE FIGURINE REPRESENTS LARAN, THE ETRUSCAN GOD OF WAR, CORRESPONDING TO THE GREEK ARES. IT DATES TO THE MID-5TH CENTURY BC (ARCHAEOLOGICAL MUSEUM, FLORENCE).

123 LEFT – THIS BRONZE VOTIVE FIGURINE REPRESENTS THE ETRUSCAN DEITY FUFLUNS, CORRESPONDING TO THE GREEK DIONYSUS (ESTENSE MUSEUM, MODENA).

123 RIGHT – THE STATUE KNOWN AS THE TODI MARS PORTRAYS AN ARMED FIGURE. IT IS AN IMPORTANT VOTIVE OFFERING FROM A LARGE SANCTUARY IN TODI (ANCIENT TUDER), OFFERED BY A HIGH-RANKING FIGURE. IT DATES TO THE LATE 5TH OR EARLY 4TH CENTURY BC (VATICAN MUSEUMS, VATICAN CITY).

124-125 - THE MOST
IMPORTANT EXAMPLE OF LARGE
ETRUSCAN BRONZES
PRODUCED IN AREZZO (LATE
5TH OR EARLY 4TH CENTURY
BC) DEPICTS A CHIMERA WITH
THE HEAD AND BODY OF A LION,
A GOAT'S HEAD ON THE BACK
AND A SNAKELIKE TAIL. IT IS
FROM THE VOTIVE DEPOSIT OF
PORTA LAURENTINA
(ARCHAEOLOGICAL MUSEUM,
AREZZO).

SEAFARING AND TRADE

As noted earlier, Livy's famous observation that "before the Roman supremacy, the power of the Tuscans [Etruscans] was widely extended both by sea and land" highlights one of Etruscans' universally acknowledged strengths: their ancient knowledge of the sea, which was superior to that of any Western population. However, reconstructing the main aspects of the Etruscans' maritime power, such as the types of ships they used, their routes and their trade practices, is no simple task, as information is fragmentary and meager.

The rare depictions of ships found on artifacts and the fortunate discovery of wrecks at the bottom of the sea are essential for reconstructing what these vessels must have looked like when Etruscan trade reached its maximum expansion in the 6th and 5th centuries BC. Approximately 65 ft (19 m) long, they were made of planking that was "sewn" together or bound with ropes. The hull terminated with a curved stern, whereas the prow was fitted with a ram (*rostrum*) to strike and sink enemy ships. The interior of the hull, sealed with pitch, held cargo that was carefully stored to optimize space. Moreover, piles of stones have been found in the wrecks, leading to the assumption that the vessels were ballasted as the goods were sold and offloaded.

In reconstructing the routes used by Etruscan merchants – who had no instrumentation whatsoever, but were extremely skilled at exploiting the dominant winds and currents – it is essential to bear in mind that they must have sailed during daytime, close to the coast in order to maintain visual contact with land. These considerations, along with the position of the wrecks that have been found and the distribution of materials on the mainland, allow us to assume that there were numerous trade routes that crossed the Mediterranean, extending in particular from the ports of the flourishing cities of Southern Etruria and from Populonia, the only Etruscan city on the coast.

The routes touched Corsica and Sardinia, and then went on to Carthage or, heading towards the Ligurian coast, they went to Provence and from here to the mouth of the Rhone, continuing to Massalia (Marseille) and Emporion (Ampurias), in Spain. Another important route headed south, hugging the coast of Latium and Campania, with moorings and points for transporting goods inland, and then continued to the Aeolian Islands, the Strait of Messina and Sicily.

Based on all available documentation, coupled with descriptions from literary and epigraphic sources, we can deduce that in the 6th century BC the Etruscans – who more than a century earlier had established profitable trade throughout the Tyrrhenian area, organized through individual procedures and overseen by high-ranking figures – began to refine their trade practices. They set up a collective system regulated by complex procedures, which included concepts such as down payments, transactions be-

fore witnesses and middlemen. However, everything was managed by merchants, who played a pivotal role in the entire organization.

This type of trade was profoundly interrelated with the societies that received the products, whose circulation was naturally connected with the simultaneous presence of different groups. Indeed, in the Archaic Mediterranean, the exchange of goods always went hand in hand with the movement of travelers or emigrants.

126-127 - THIS AERIAL VIEW SHOWS THE SITE OF GRAVISCA, THE PORT OF TARQUINIA.

127 BOTTOM - THE CYLINDRICAL IMPASTO VESSEL WITH A LID (PYX) IS ORNATELY DECORATED WITH WHITE PAINT. THE SIDE SHOWN HERE DEPICTS A NAVAL BATTLE IN WHICH TWO SHIPS, DRIVEN BY OARSMEN, ARE ATTACKING EACH OTHER. THE BOW OF THE SHIP ON THE LEFT IS SHAPED LIKE THE HEAD OF A FISH, WHILE THE ONE ON THE RIGHT IS SHAPED LIKE A SWAN'S HEAD. THIS OBJECT IS FROM CERVETERI AND DATES TO THE LATE 7TH CENTURY BC (LOUVRE MUSEUM, PARIS).

MARKETPLACES: PORTS AND EMPORIUMS

In addition to their skills as shipbuilders and seafarers, the Etruscans also executed impressive works of hydraulic engineering to modify the coastline and create perfectly organized port areas that were connected to the cities close to the Tyrrhenian Sea. They also planned a string of ports of calls and landing places on the Tyrrhenian coast that were settled by Etruscan traders, establishing a network of bases to support navigation and distribution centers to transport goods to inland areas. With the development of the urban model in the first few decades of the 6th century BC, trade also came under the auspices of the city-state. This meant that trade was managed by the large production class that can be recognized in political and religious institutions, and that wanted to work with other trade circuits in the Mediterranean. As a result, simple landing places were transformed into ports with a standard structure, which were organized according to the Mediterranean model of the emporium, setting up port installations that were closely overseen by civic power. Large sanctuaries were built at the ports to guarantee the safety and protection of foreign merchants – in exchange for part of their revenues – and provide them with a place to stay. Thus, the city-state guaranteed the redistribution of imported products, as clearly indicated by discoveries at Pyrgi (the port of Cerveteri) and Regisvilla (the port of Vulci). This is also evident from the extraordinary findings from Gravisca, the emporium of Tarquinia, where materials concentrated chiefly in the sanctuary accurately reflect the enormous number of Greek artifacts found at the necropolis and in the settlement. These sites were transformed from trading areas into places in which the lifestyles and ideolo-

gies of foreign partners were passed on to the local communities. As in the past, the Greek culture represented a significant model of prestige. This sparked a "second Hellenization" process that had an even more profound effect than the contact established with the Euboeans at the beginning of the 8th century BC, despite the fact that these earlier dealings had led to the acquisition of instruments, technologies, ideologies and lifestyles, and the influx of Phoenician and Levantine goods that had characterized the great proto-urban centers of the 7th century BC. In short, the vehicles for this process were the merchants and artisans of eastern Greece, who were then integrated to a certain extent as metics in the urban communities. Natives of Samos, Miletus and Phocaea, they arrived together with a varied group of individuals who must have patronized the emporiums of the 6th century BC. Following the conquest of Ionia in 545 BC by King Cyrus of Persia, others also fled to places such as Etruria that were willing to take them in and offer them an opportunity to reestablish their business and trade. The Near Eastern influence was replaced by elements brought in from Aegina, a Greek island in the Aegean Sea that flourished thanks to crafts and commerce, leading to great colonial expansion. The Greek historian Herodotus described Sostratos, an Aeginian merchant who had amassed great wealth. This information is confirmed by the presence of an anchor stock that Sostratos dedicated to Apollo of Aegina at the sanctuary of Gravisca. Archaeological evidence provides tangible proof of these trade relations: a vast quantity of imported pottery has been discovered in the settlements and the necropolises of Cerveteri, Vulci and Tarquinia – to name just a few areas – in which rich burials were accompanied by numerous fur-

128 LEFT - THE CAERETAN HYDRIA WAS MADE BY CRAFTSMEN FROM EASTERN GREECE. THIS BLACK-FIGURE VESSEL DEPICTS TWO EAGLES IN FLIGHT AND A SMALL HARE. ATTRIBUTED TO THE EAGLE PAINTER, IT WAS MADE IN THE LATE 6TH CENTURY BC (LOUVRE MUSEUM, PARIS).

128 RIGHT - THE LARGE KRATER KNOWN AS THE "FRANÇOIS VASE" – AFTER ITS DISCOVERER – IS A MASTERPIECE OF BLACK-FIGURE POTTERY. IT WAS MADE IN ATHENS BY THE POTTER ERGOTISMOS AND WAS PAINTED BY KLEITIAS IN THE MID-6TH CENTURY BC. THE KRATER WAS FOUND IN A RICH TOMB NEAR MODERN-DAY CHIUSI (ARCHAEOLOGICAL MUSEUM, FLORENCE).

nishings, predominantly pottery from different Ionian and Greek workshops. Vessels/vases such as shipping amphorae made in eastern Greece, Chios, Corinth and Attica confirm the ongoing importation of Greek wine in the 6th century BC. However, tableware and ceremonial artifacts bearing figured decorations that were extremely popular in Etruria play an even more significant role, due to the amount and the quality of information they have yielded. It is also important to emphasize the key role of pottery in archaeological studies. On the one hand, this production is fundamental for analyzing crafts and trade trends. At the same time pottery is indispensable for studying and understanding the mental processes of the ancient societies that produced them. As far as the Etruscan world is concerned, the pottery imported from Greece was unquestionably a factor that accelerated Hellenic acculturation. Pottery produced in Corinth was one of the luxury goods made for the well-to-do classes. These artifacts have been found in Etruscan contexts spanning nearly 200 years, up to the mid-6th century BC, when these wares became so popular that local workshops were established to produce imitations. The pottery from eastern Greece is equally interesting. These items were produced in centers on the coast of Asia Minor and the nearby Greek islands, such as Samos, Rhodes and Chios, and were imported above all between the last quarter of the 7th century and the middle of the 6th century BC. They were categorized mainly as drinking vessels, such as the famous "Ionian cups," and bottles for scented oils and fragrances. These two categories were so fashionable among the Etruscans that imitations were produced locally. It is no accident that groups of Ionian craftsmen settled in Cerveteri, making objects such as the Campana dinoi and the Caeretan hydriae, which had a decisive influence on the development of arts and crafts. Similarly, the painters who frescoed some of the chamber tombs at Tarquinia were Ionian. Above all, however, the most widely represented pottery was the type produced in Athens starting in the early 6th century BC. Distinguished by reddish clay, it was richly decorated with black figures and, as of the second half of the 6th century BC, red figures. Tangible proof of the demand for highly decorative Attic products among the Etruscan elites comes from one of the most monumental vases to come down to us from antiquity: the François krater. Signed by Kleitas as painter and Ergotimos as potter, the krater, which dates back to about 570 BC, was commissioned or received as an extraordinarily valuable precious gift by an aristocrat from Chiusi. The widespread presence of such vessels makes them highly significant. First of all, they were the main media for transmitting Hellenic iconographies and thus the knowledge connected with them, such as myths and epics, which contributed

decisively to the acculturation process of the ruling elites who commissioned and purchased these works. Secondly, so many specimens have been found at Etruscan necropolises that it has been possible to draw up a chronology for these items. As a result, they provide compelling evidence for reconstructing the historical events, arts and crafts of the Greek civilization and of the other cultures that were active around the Mediterranean. Another very intriguing aspect that sheds light on Archaic trade processes and the impact of Etruscan customers on Attic production involves the vases that the Athenian workshops made specifically for the Tyrrhenian clientele, such as the type known as "Tyrrhenian amphorae" and, later, commissioned or "bespoke" vases. There were also Attic workshops that were in direct contact with the means of distribution and thus specialized in pottery forms that were not part of the Greek repertory, such as Nicosthenic amphorae, which reproduced the forms typical of bucchero ware. There was such an enormous demand – for example, in the mid-6th century BC Vulci acquired more Attic products than the most important Greek cities – that craftsmen from the Kerameikos at Athens came to Etruria. This influx stimulated local workshops, which produced imitations, although other works were also profoundly influenced. Attic vases were imported in quantities that varied depending on the period and the cities involved, on the relationship between the individual Etruscan communities and their Greek partners. Attic imports to Southern Etruria declined following the Battle of Cumae, due to an internal economic crisis that led to the closure of market areas and a change in trade routes. The Syracusans' victory over the Etruscans at Cumae in 474 BC and then again off Elba in 453–452 put Etruria at a disadvantage, although the political and military repercussions outweighed the economic ones. The cities of Southern Etruria bore the brunt of this, with a dramatic decrease in the importation of Attic pottery. However, the economic deficit of these territories was offset by the prosperity of the cities in the central and northern areas, as demonstrated by the redistribution of Vulcian bronzes by the emporium at Spina. From Spina, these goods crossed the Ticino River and were transported through the Rhine basin and into central Europe. During this period, Padan Etruria – with the two emporiums of Adria and Spina – was part of a significant circulation of goods, with Greek ships that brought in high-quality pottery in exchange for the abundant agricultural products from the inland, particularly grains. The upper Tyrrhenian coast, particularly the area around Populonia, seems to have been involved in trade and was receptive to it, as demonstrated by the city's first silver issues. Coupled with those of Volterra, they point to an attempt to simplify trade in a highly dynamic area.

130 LEFT AND 131 - THE TWO ATTIC BLACK-FIGURE AMPHORAE ARE FROM VULCI AND DATE BACK TO THE 6TH CENTURY BC (LOUVRE MUSEUM, PARIS).

130 RIGHT - THE ATTIC BLACK-FIGURE HYDRIA FROM VULCI WAS MADE IN THE LATE 6TH CENTURY BC (LOUVRE MUSEUM, PARIS).

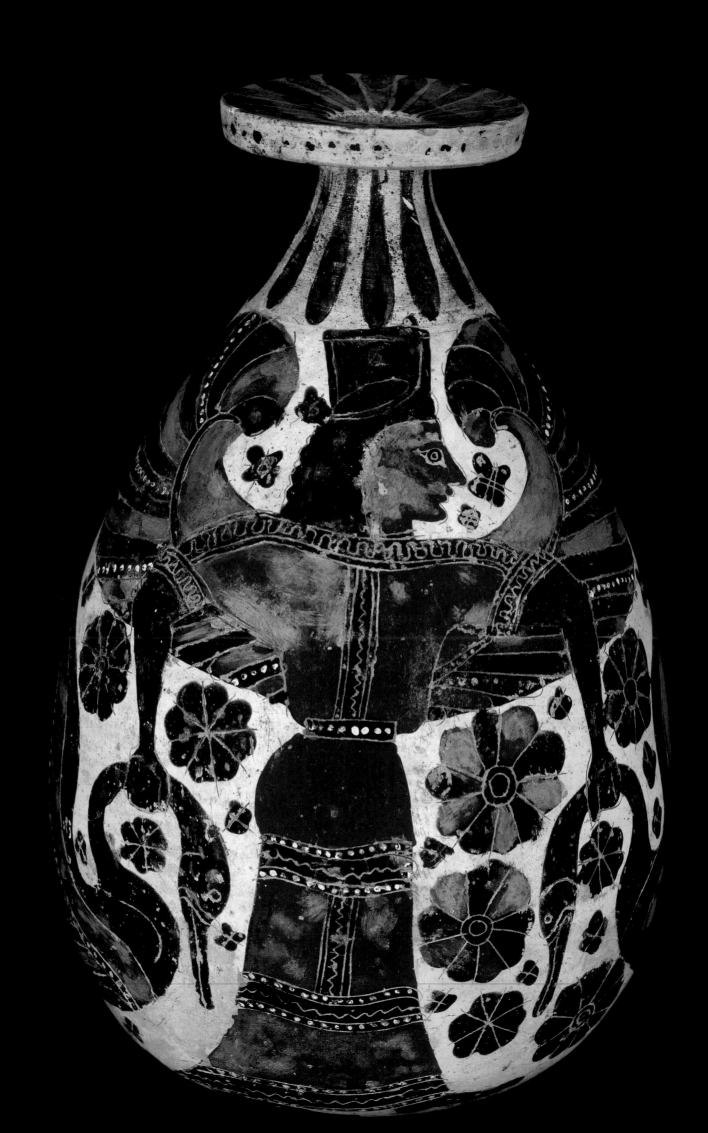

The new urban layout and significant population increase that occurred in the cities, which were fully formed during the 6th century BC, led to new ways of exploiting resources through more organized production systems that strived to meet growing domestic consumption and create the surpluses needed for trade.

The exploitation of metal, which had always been critical to the Etruscan economy, benefited from new mining, workmanship and refining processes involving local manpower and technological innovations. All of these aspects are amply demonstrated by findings from the settlement close to the ore deposits near Lake Accesa and from the suburban district of Populonia. The latter excavation has also confirmed the existence of the well-made furnaces discussed by Diodorus Siculus in a passage about Etruscan metalworking.

The cities, which had developed into important areas of consumption by this time, were forced to upgrade the territories they controlled, transforming them into rural areas under their rule. To achieve this, the political authorities embarked on a great community effort to organize important water drainage and management works, and eloquent evidence of this remain at the sites of Veii, Cerveteri, Orvieto and Chiusi.

Vast networks of wells and tunnels – *cuniculi* – were dug for various purposes, depending on the site and the type of soil: to drain the land by damming and controlling springs and brooks; to collect and save rainwater; and to assure water supplies by tapping into water tables.

These ingeniously devised hydraulic works and cultivation methods reflect very ancient knowledge, such as the practice of fallowing fields, learned when the Etruscans first came into contact with the Greeks. They thus increased the fertility of these lands, which was described by a number of ancient sources. For example, the Greek historian Diodorus Siculus wrote that the Etruscans occupied areas that produced every type of crop, noting that they had abundant harvests because they worked the land so intensively.

This led to the widespread cultivation of grains that, through increasingly improved means of production, led to the formation of surpluses. In a famous passage by Dionysius of Halicarnassus, the historian observed that the Etruscan cities offered supplies to Rome during the famines of the 5th century BC.

In the 7th century BC, and particularly during the 6th and 5th centuries, the Etruscans also turned to the intensive cultivation of grapes and olives, for which the heavy soils characterized by a rocky or limestone base, typical of Etruria, were ideal.

These types of production required specialized labor and rapidly became speculative in nature, developing in the relation not only to growing wealth and prosperity, in which prestige was emphasized by drinking precious beverages such as wine and using fragrant ointments made with oil, but also to the sale of surpluses, as demonstrated by the distribution of bucchero and clay vessels, i.e., amphorae for shipping wine and containers for scented oils.

132 - This precious vase (alabastron), made in Corinth to hold scented oils, is from Cerveteri. The decoration depicts a winged goddess who is holding two birds by the neck (Louvre Museum, Paris).

133 - A dancing figure in a padded costume (komast), surrounded by floral elements, decorates one side of a Corinthian alabastron from Cerveteri, which dates to the late 7th century BC (Louvre Museum, Paris).

During this period, trade activities were organized systematically, above all for wine, of which Etruria was the leading exporter in the western Mediterranean until the second half of the 6th century. The distribution of wine went hand in hand with the sale of bucchero ware and Corinthian-Etruscan pottery items related to drinking rituals.

Bucchero ware and Corinthian-Etruscan pottery fully exemplify an aspect of the crafts of the 6th century BC, which included not only high-quality products for a narrower circle of wealthy and demanding customers, but also artifacts made on a larger scale for exportation and to cater to middling demand. Large quantities of these commonplace objects were produced, confirming the presence of emerging urban classes that were in a position to acquire such items. To satisfy this demand, each city had its own medium-level workshops, with artisans who operated in small groups under the guidance of a shop head. These workshops produced consumer goods such as bucchero ware, painted pottery, utensils and metal furnishings.

Findings from necropolises as well as settlements reveal the gradual emergence of consumer objects that were produced on a large scale, with standardized processes that included the use of molds or rollers. Examples include the pithoi to contain foodstuffs and braziers used for heating. This red impasto ware, which was decorated with a flat stamp or a decorative band impressed with a small cylinder, was typical of Cerveteri's production until the mid-6th century BC.

Nevertheless, bucchero ware was the most important type of pottery. This Etruscan ware had a distinctive black finish that was probably achieved by firing the pottery in a smoky atmosphere that, at certain temperatures, transformed the clay's ferric oxide, which is red, into ferrous oxide, which is black. The walls of the vases, which were initially very thin (*bucchero sottile*), gradually became thicker in the early 6th century BC, when bucchero ware became increasingly widespread and was exported throughout the Mediterranean, in a repertory of forms tied to ritual drinking practices.

Although these items were originally produced in Southern Etruria, during the 6th century BC workshops in the cities of Northern and Central Etruria began to make them as well. One of the most important producers was Chiusi, which played a fundamental role in the production of heavy bucchero (*bucchero pesante*). This type was distinguished by thicker walls and new stamp-decorated forms, with rich sculptural appendages on the handles or, in common items, with miniature decorations created with a cylinder stamp. In burials, bucchero – considered prized ware – was not deposited as individual objects but as complete "table sets" composed of numerous pieces.

Corinthian-Etruscan pottery – i.e., made in Etruria to imitate Corinthian pottery – was also widespread. It was made chiefly in Southern Etruria and along the coasts starting in the late 7th century BC, and included high-quality items. The production of tableware and vessels to hold scented oil commenced in the 6th century BC and, along with bucchero ware, these items were exported throughout the Mediterranean. However, large quantities, in a variety of forms, were also used in burials and votive settings until the second half of the 6th century, when they became obsolete.

135 LEFT - THE BUCCHERO CUP IS DECORATED WITH A FRIEZE OF ANIMALS IMPRESSED USING A ROLLER STAMP WHILE THE CLAY WAS STILL WET. IT WAS PROBABLY MADE IN TARQUINIA AND DATES TO THE FIRST HALF OF THE 6TH CENTURY BC (BRITISH MUSEUM, LONDON).

135 RIGHT - THIS VASE IS A BUCCHERO OINOCHOE DECORATED WITH PARALLEL FRIEZES THAT ARE DIVIDED BY FILLETS, WITH REAL AND IMAGINARY FIGURES IN RELIEF. THE ARTIFACT DATES TO THE FIRST HALF OF THE 6TH CENTURY BC (LOUVRE MUSEUM, PARIS).

136-137 - THE BUCCHERO BRAZIER
(FOCULUS) IS DECORATED WITH THE HEADS
OF WOMEN AND IMAGINARY CREATURES,
RENDERED IN RELIEF; THE FEET OF THE
BRAZIER ARE SHAPED LIKE THE PAWS OF A
LION. IT WAS MADE IN CHIUSI IN THE 6TH
CENTURY BC (LOUVRE MUSEUM, PARIS).

137 RIGHT - THE BUCCHERO CUP ON A TALL
BASE, RICHLY DECORATED IN RELIEF, WAS
MADE DURING THE FIRST HALF OF THE 6TH
CENTURY BC (LOUVRE MUSEUM, PARIS).

Bronze works began to be produced on a large scale in the 6th century BC. They were made chiefly in cities with a long tradition in this field, such as Vulci and Populonia. These centers made high-quality objects, but they were always mass-produced as sets. Tripods, candelabra, thymiateria, objects for symposia and lebetes were very common in burials, and were also exported in large quantities. Indeed, the bronze furnishings produced in Etruria must have been famous, for Critias, a leading Athenian poet of the late 5th century BC, praised their quality.

The high level of quality of the Vulcian bronzes is beautifully demonstrated by the furnishings from the Tomb of the Warrior at Vulci, dating back to the last two decades of the 6th century BC. The tomb yielded heavy armor as well as a set of bronze symposium objects and a set of Attic vases, including a Panathenaic amphora. This prestigious prize, which was awarded at the Panathenaic Games, thus glorified the dead man's athletic prowess.

These furnishings, along with the rich panoply (complete armor), also bear witness to the circulation of hoplite tactics and equipment, which replaced the hand-to-hand combat typical of the Archaic period. As a result, these items emphasized the power of attacking as a group, in accordance with the egalitarian organization that distinguished urban society in the 6th century BC.

138 - THIS PRECIOUS BRONZE JUG (OINOCHOE) HAS A THREE-LOBED SPOUT AND A FLAT VERTICAL HANDLE WITH DENSE RIBBING AND TWO ROSETTES ON THE SIDES. IT IS FROM THE TOMB OF THE FLABELLA AT POPULONIA AND DATES TO THE FIRST HALF OF THE 6TH CENTURY BC (ARCHAEOLOGICAL MUSEUM, FLORENCE).

139 - THIS REPOUSSÉ BRONZE PLATE, PROBABLY THE CHEEK GUARD OF A HELMET OR PART OF A SHIELD GRIP, WAS PART OF THE PANOPLY OF AN ETRUSCAN HOPLITE BURIED IN A CHAMBER TOMB KNOWN AS THE TOMB OF THE WARRIOR, DISCOVERED AT THE VULCI NECROPOLIS (VILLA GIULIA NATIONAL ETRUSCAN MUSEUM, ROME).

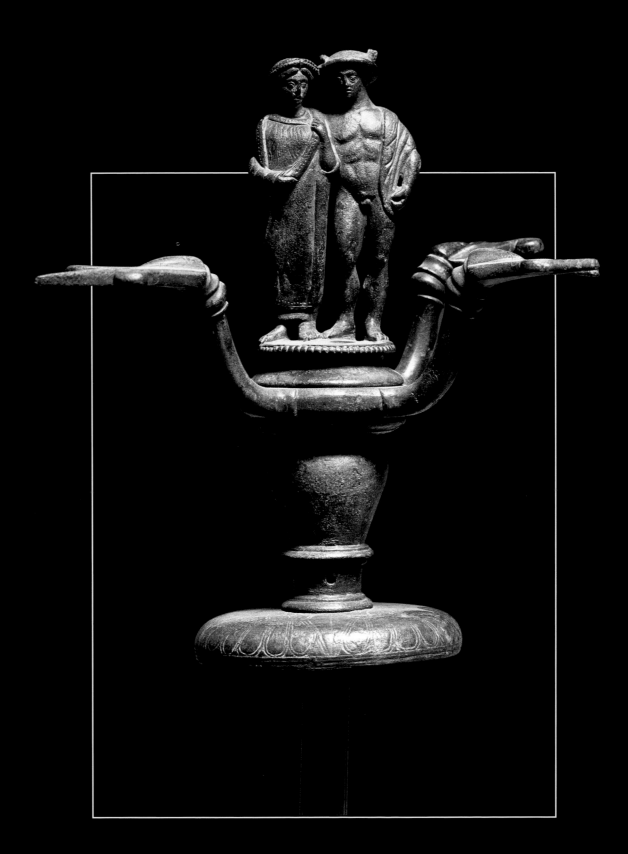

140 - THE BRONZE CANDELABRUM WITH THE FIGURES OF HERMES AND PSYCHE WAS PROBABLY MADE IN VULCI IN THE MID-5TH CENTURY BC (ARCHAEOLOGICAL MUSEUM, FERRARA).

141 - THE TWO-HEADED BRONZE VASE, DEPICTING A MAENAD AND A SATYR, WAS MADE BETWEEN THE 5TH AND 4TH CENTURIES BC (THE HERMITAGE, ST. PETERSBURG).

Figured pottery is another extremely important part of the artisanal production of the Archaic period. In cities, the considerable number of vessels produced at various Greek locations, coupled with the establishment of workshops entrusted to foreign workers, first from Ionia and then from Athens, helped renew local pottery production. Like all other crafts, pottery was profoundly influenced by the enormous array of iconographies, sagas and myths that had reached Etruria.

The production of Etruscan black-figure pottery commenced in the mid-6th century BC and was commissioned by high-ranking customers. The Greek sagas, which fascinated the Etruscans, were used extensively in the decorative repertory and, in some cases, they were reinterpreted based on local traditions.

Numerous workshops produced black-figure pottery in the main cities between the mid-6th and mid-5th centuries BC. One of them was that of the Micali Painter, who produced the largest number of objects. His vast production included not only figured vases decorated with fantastic animals and dance, battle and mythological scenes, but also vases bearing only floral motifs and a series of items that constantly repeated the same decorative patterns.

Influenced by Attic pottery that continued to be imported to Etruria, during the 6th century BC Etruscan workshops acquired the red-figure technique, producing large quantities of these wares. Several workshops put out top-quality items, but soon this type of pottery became very standardized.

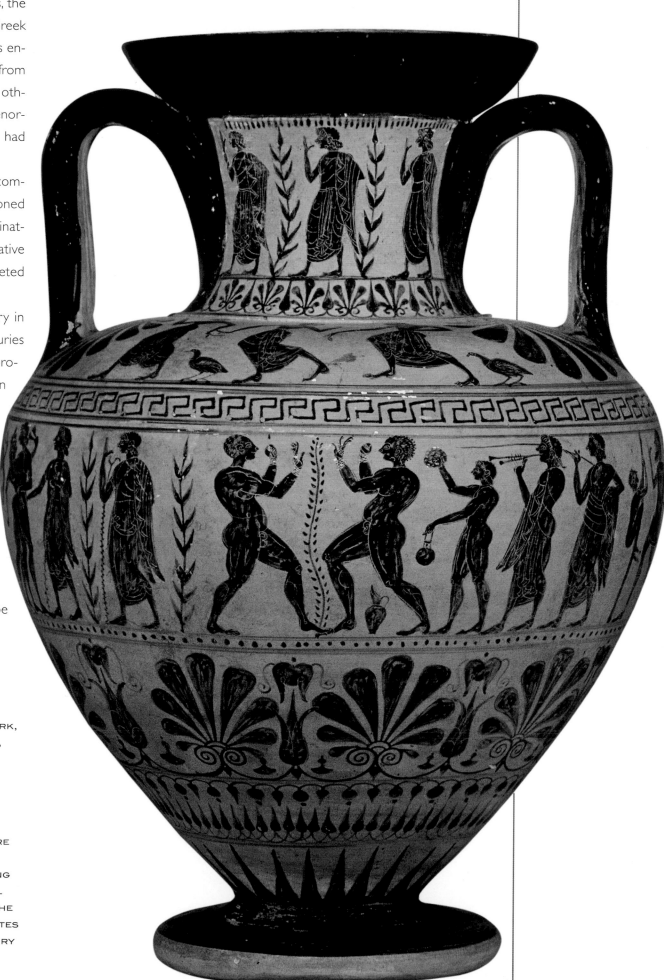

142 LEFT - THIS BLACK-FIGURE WATER JAR (HYDRIA), THE WORK OF THE MICALI PAINTER, IS DECORATED WITH TWO FRIEZES DEPICTING A MIXTURE OF MYTHOLOGICAL AND REAL SCENES. IT WAS PROBABLY MADE IN VULCI IN THE LATE 6TH CENTURY BC (BRITISH MUSEUM, LONDON).

142 RIGHT - THIS BLACK-FIGURE AMPHORA DEPICTS A SERIES OF NUDE MALE FIGURES RUNNING FROM RIGHT TO LEFT. THIS WORK, BY THE MICALI PAINTER, DATES TO THE LATE 6TH CENTURY BC (ARCHAEOLOGICAL MUSEUM, TARQUINIA).

143 - THIS BLACK-FIGURE AMPHORA, WHOSE MAIN FRIEZE DEPICTS SPORTING EVENTS AND THEATRICAL ENTERTAINMENT, IS BY THE MICALI PAINTER AND DATES TO THE LATE 6TH CENTURY BC (BRITISH MUSEUM, LONDON).

ARISTOCRATS AND THE WEALTHY: LIFE AND DEATH

In the Villanovan period, the nascent aristocracies reaffirmed the opulence and values of their status by depositing furnishings, sacrificing the objects of the deceased and transporting their bodies, as part of a series of rituals with powerful ideological underpinnings. The princes of the large urban centers of the Orientalizing period were manifestly intrigued by the monarchies of the Near East, adopting all the prestige goods that reached Etruria and displaying them during ceremonies and in burials, which achieved levels of extraordinary richness and complex rituality during the 7th century BC.

In the 6th century BC, the influx of goods and merchants from the cities of eastern Greece had a decisive influence on the Etruscan mentality and culture. Among the aristocracy, it led to the adoption of lifestyles revolving around luxury and the display of wealth — characteristics of the opulent societies of Asia Minor — and this was highly visible in aspects connected with funerary rituals. Aristocrats and the well-to-do spared no effort in building and furnishing the houses of the dead, performing funeral rituals, organizing elaborate athletic contests, horse races and spectacles for funerals, and depositing tomb furnishings that included a rich array of vessels, jewelry and bronzes.

Nevertheless, the display of excess and sophisticated customs also affected daily life, as we can glean from Greek literature. These sources, which were openly critical of these practices, described the amount and quality of food served in prized vessels, the sumptuous furnishings, the beautiful garb and appearance of servants and, above all, the presence of women in convivial moments when, reclining alongside their husbands, they would participate in banquets. This type of scene is exquisitely depicted on the Sarcophagus of the Spouses, a terracotta masterpiece from Cerveteri dating from this period.

144 AND 145 - THE UNDISPUTED MASTERPIECE OF IONIC-STYLE CAERETAN TERRACOTTA SCULPTURE, THE SARCOPHAGUS OF THE SPOUSES IS AN ENORMOUS CINERARY URN MADE IN THE SHAPE OF A KLINE WITH THE COUPLE TAKING PART IN A BANQUET. THIS EXQUISITELY CRAFTED ARTIFACT, DISTINGUISHED BY SOFT, SUPPLE SURFACES, WAS MADE IN THE LATE 6TH CENTURY BC. THE INTRICATE AND WELL-DEFINED RENDERING OF THE HAIR AND THE FOLDS OF THE GARMENTS ARE CLEARLY EVIDENT ON THE BACK (VILLA GIULIA NATIONAL ETRUSCAN MUSEUM, ROME).

In effect, the extraordinary arts and crafts of the 6th and 5th centuries BC give us great insight into this extraordinary side of Etruscan life, which is so eloquently illustrated in the famous paintings that decorated the tombs of Tarquinia.

Painted tombs represent a very small percentage of the total burials at Tarquinia and thus reflect a very restricted group of élites. They were chamber tombs with a pitched roof, in which the upper part of the wall, which rose from a plinth, the gable and the two slopes of the roof were covered with paintings, some of which creating extraordinary illusions. For

example, in the Tomb of the Lionesses and the Tomb of the Hunter, it seems as if one is outdoors, under a pavilion made of wooden beams and lined with fabrics so sheer that the surrounding landscape is visible. In some cases, a closed door was painted on the back wall to represent the division between life and death, and make it clear to the observer that the events were not taking place in the afterlife.

The figured friezes reflected the eastern Greek style adopted by the Etruscan aristocracies. They included athletic contests, chariot races, equestrian exercises, dances and music, as well as typical local entertainment and figures. This varied set of figurations decorating the focal point of the representation – the back wall – was replaced in the late 6th century BC by the banquet scene, which became the central theme of the decoration, around which all the other works revolved.

It is important to underscore that the interpretation of these subjects can be vague in some cases, leading to great uncertainty. In fact, some scenes seem to suggest events from real life, yet they can also be interpreted as moments projected into otherworldly dimensions. Regardless of whether we consider the banquet and games as moments in the "social" life and pastimes of aristocrats or as aspects closely linked with

the funerary ritual, the choice of different figurations may hold more complex messages tied to the desire of the deceased and of the group to portray themselves, their expectations and their fears in a specific way and through given symbols.

One of the most extraordinary phases in all of Western painting commenced in approximately 530 BC. With the arrival of craftsmen from eastern Greece, Etruscan aristocrats chose to satisfy their celebratory needs by commissioning figured cycles from the best decorators of the era. Taking up a tradition already present in Etruria – as seen in paintings from

the mid-7th century BC with figures of real or mythological animals – these artists began to paint more intricate scenes on tomb walls. These works show clear-cut similarities with coeval pottery produced locally, likewise by Ionian artists and hence permitting direct comparisons.

The contribution of these artisans also emerged in the adoption of a new technique. The walls were smoothed and covered with a layer of plaster that was enriched with substances to slow the drying process. The plaster was then whitewashed to form a ground on which the preparatory drawing was incised with a stylus. The painting was then created rather rapidly with a highly varied palette, using red, black, brown and yellow, with the addition of green and blue.

Each of the frescoed tombs is astonishing, with highly realistic images, bold colors and figurations that draw the observer into the world of the Etruscans.

The Tomb of the Bulls is unique, as it depicts a scene from Homer's saga – the only example prior to the 4th century BC – in which Achilles' ambush of Troilus clearly conveys a message celebrating the heroic virtues of the young Trojan prince, to whom the deceased is compared.

In the Tomb of the Augurs, alongside a group of athletes

who are boxing and wrestling (the prizes are represented by large bronze *lebetes*), there are also masked figures involved in ritual games exclusive to the Etruscan world, such as the duel between Phersu and a naked man with a sack over his head. The form of entertainment portrayed in the Tomb of the Jugglers is also clearly local. This work features dancers moving to the music of a *syrinx* (pan pipes), with an extraordinary female figure dressed in a sheer gown. Games are also depicted at the Tomb of the Olympiad, but in this case they are Greek, and a lively *biga* (two-horse chariot) race is portrayed.

146 LEFT - THE BACK WALL OF THE TOMB OF THE LIONESSES (530-520 BC) FROM THE MONTEROZZI NECROPOLIS IN TARQUINIA IS PAINTED WITH FIGURES OF MUSICIANS AND DANCERS. THE LARGE KRATER AWARDED AS A PRIZE AT GAMES IS DEPICTED IN THE MIDDLE AND FROLICKING DOLPHINS ARE PORTRAYED ALONG THE LOWER BAND.

146 RIGHT - THE WORK ON THE SIDE WALL OF THE TOMB OF LIONESSES PORTRAYS A MAN BANQUETING, SET OVER A FRIEZE OF STYLIZED WAVES.

146-147 - A DANCING MALE AND A RICHLY GARBED FEMALE DANCER ARE PAINTED ON THE BACK WALL OF THE TOMB OF THE LIONESSES.

148 - THE UPPER BAND OF THE BACK
WALL OF THE TOMB OF THE BULLS
(540 BC), AT THE MONTEROZZI
NECROPOLIS, DEPICTS SEVERAL
EROTIC SCENES.

148-149 - THE CLOSE-UP OF THE BACK
WALL IN THE MIDDLE ROOM OF THE
TOMB OF THE BULLS SHOWS THE
UPPER FRIEZE PORTRAYING AN
EPISODE FROM THE *ILIAD*: ACHILLES
AMBUSHING TROILUS.

150 TOP - A DANCER IN A SHEER DRESS, ACCOMPANIED BY MUSICIANS, IS DEPICTED IN THE TOMB OF THE JUGGLERS AT TARQUINIA, DATED 530 BC.

150 CENTER - THIS PHOTOGRAPH SHOWS AN OVERVIEW OF THE TOMB OF THE AUGURS AT TARQUINIA.

150 BOTTOM - THE PAINTINGS AT THE TOMB OF THE JUGGLERS ILLUSTRATE THE FUNERARY GAMES HELD TO HONOR THE DEAD.

151 - THE PAINTINGS ON THE RIGHT-HAND WALL OF THE TOMB OF THE AUGURS AT TARQUINIA PORTRAY A MAN WITH A YOUNG SERVANT.

At the Fowling and Fishing Tomb, the symposium, portrayed on the gable, is coupled with a hunting scene to evoke the patrician status of the deceased.

The walls are completely covered by a sweeping marine panorama with brightly colored fish and birds, in which div-

ing and water symbolize "change" and "transition." The sea waves represented at the Tomb of the Lionesses have the same significance.

In the early 5th century BC, the panorama of Tarquinian painting changed with the great transormation of this late Archaic phase, in which the theme of the symposium – painted so far on the gable as a secondary element – was highlighted through its placement on the back wall, with

dancers and musicians, amidst trees, portrayed along the sides. Evidently, the change in the social status of customers inspired them to make specific choices from a variety of themes that had previously been far more extensive and were designed to glorify wealth and opulence. Thus, the indispensable elements of the funerary setting were codified in banqueting scenes and the portrayal of dancers and musicians.

152 top - The scene of the diver is painted in the second chamber of the Fowling and Fishing Tomb at Tarquinia.

152 bottom and 152-153 - The pediment of the back wall of the Fowling and Fishing Tomb depicts a banquet; the paintings on the wall portray fishermen and a hunter aiming a sling at birds in flight.

153 bottom - The pediment of the first chamber of the Fowling and Fishing Tomb is decorated with plant motifs, wreaths, and men on foot and on horseback.

The painter of the Tomb of the Bigas can be credited with adopting a model that was destined to span a century. The banquet scene, which takes place outdoors, accompanied by musicians and dancers, may have been chosen to display the patron's sophistication and wealth. The competitive scenes, represented in front of a U-shaped gallery, are instead relegated to the smaller frieze, in which the fact that the athletes were naked may indicate that the young men were slaves.

This pattern is repeated in other tombs, each of which has unique characteristics. One example is the Tomb of the Leopards, named after the two majestic animals reproduced

on the gable. They seem to oversee two processions with donors, dancers and musicians playing different instruments, who converge towards the back wall where the symposium is taking place.

In the Tomb of the Funerary Bed, the representation, dominated by an enormous and powerfully symbolic empty bed, takes place under a large *velarium* (shade-providing cloth screen) whose draped edges are depicted along the walls, suggesting that the observer is outdoors. At the Tomb of the Triclinium, the canonical motif of the banquet and dancers is rendered with rich stylistic touches: a foreshortened *kline* is depicted with the same skill and technique as the motifs found on the Attic cups from this period.

At the Tomb of the Ship, the lateral space is opened up by a seascape with ships. The male figure – possible the owner of the tomb – is an aristocrat connected with overseas trade who is contemplating one of the vessels used for his business.

154 - THIS OVERALL VIEW SHOWS TWO WALLS AND THE CHECKERBOARD CEILING FROM THE TOMB OF THE TRICLINIUM, COMPLETED BETWEEN 480 AND 470 BC AT THE MONTEROZZI NECROPOLIS (TARQUINIA).

154-155 - THE CLOSE-UP FROM THE TOMB OF THE LEOPARDS AT THE MONTEROZZI NECROPOLIS IN TARQUINIA (480-470 BC) DEPICTS A FIGURE PLAYING A DOUBLE FLUTE AND A MAN HOLDING A LARGE CUP.

155 TOP - THE SIDE WALL OF THE TOMB OF THE TRICLINIUM AT THE MONTEROZZI NECROPOLIS IN TARQUINIA BEARS THE PORTRAIT OF A DANCER. THE TOMB WAS BUILT BETWEEN 480 AND 470 BC.

155 BOTTOM - THE SCENE ON THE BACK WALL OF THE TOMB OF THE LEOPARDS SHOWS FIGURES AT A BANQUET. DEPICTED IN THE PEDIMENT OVER IT ARE TWO FACING LEOPARDS WITH PLANTS ALONG THE SIDES.

156-157 - This close-up of the back wall of the Tomb of the Baron at the Monterozzi necropolis in Tarquinia, built in 520 BC, depicts a man, accompanied by an athlete offering a cup, who is encountering a woman wrapped in a mantle that covers her head. It is a parting scene: the husband is bidding his dead wife farewell.

157 top - This parting scene, with a woman in the middle, is from the Tomb of the Baron (Tarquinia).

157 bottom - The horseman, possible one of the Dioscuri, is depicted in a parting scene painted on the back wall of the Tomb of the Baron.

158 - This bearded head is a part of a cinerary statue made of tuff known as the Pluto (Archaeological Museum, Palermo).

159 - This funerary *cippus* from Chiusi is decorated with a dance scene (Archaeological Museum, Palermo).

160-161 - This funerary *cippus* from Chiusi depicts a triga race (Archaeological Museum, Palermo).

However, the Tarquinian aristocrats were not the only ones who loved to evoke their lifestyle. During the Archaic period the urbanized society of Chiusi developed a type of burial marker, the *cippus*, portraying all the scenes of the solemnities involved in the journey to the afterlife. As was the case with the tomb paintings, here too banquets, games, athletic contests, musicians and dancers provide vivid insight into the lifestyle of those who commissioned these works.

The images of women seated on chairs with armrests and male figures reclining at banquets, with women or demons nearby, represent yet another aristocratic portrayal of the banqueting scene.

This type was present in the area around Chiusi in the 5th century BC. The heads, which were movable, served as lids on the hollow bodies of the statues used to hold the ashes of the deceased.

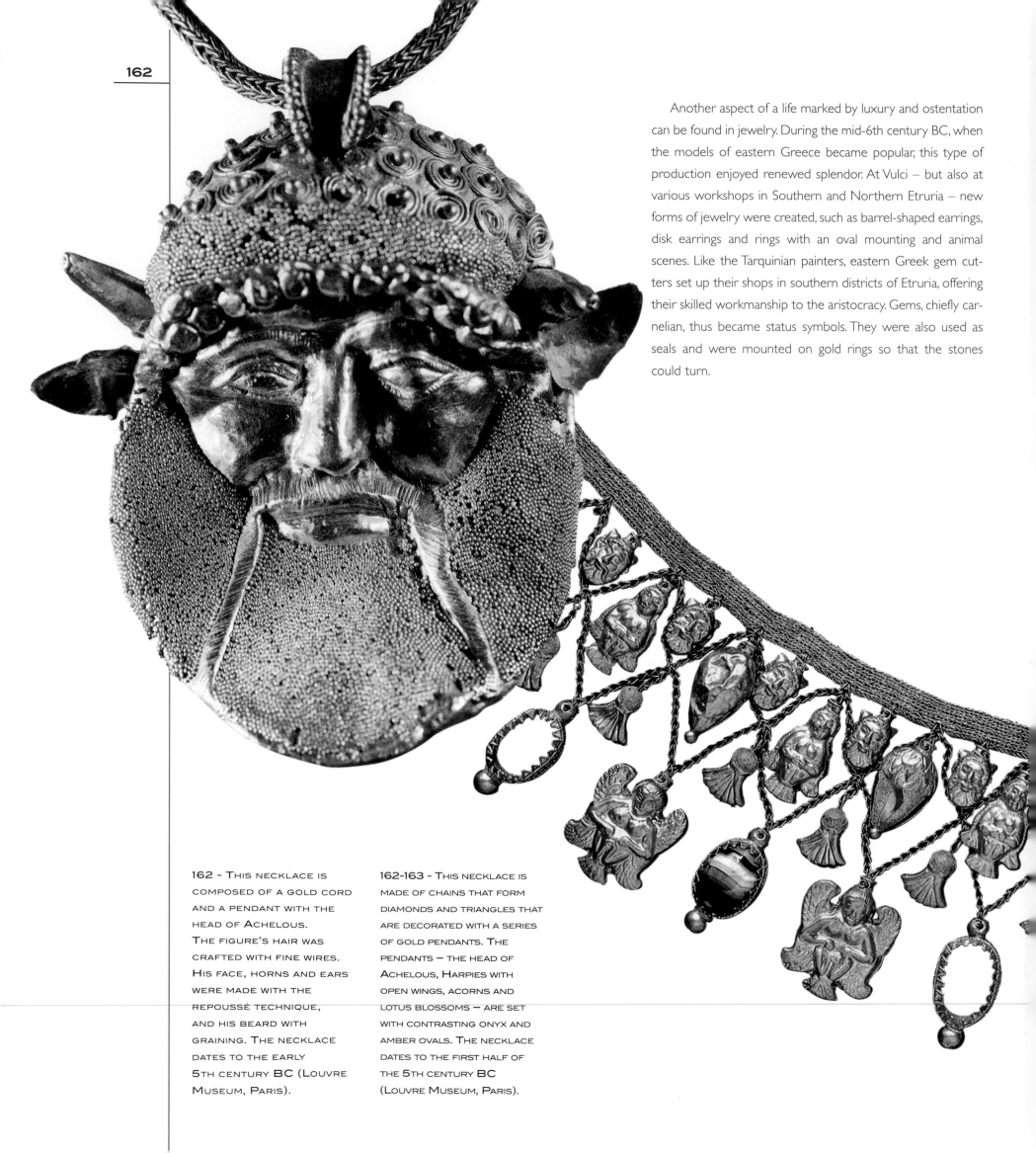

Another aspect of a life marked by luxury and ostentation can be found in jewelry. During the mid-6th century BC, when the models of eastern Greece became popular, this type of production enjoyed renewed splendor. At Vulci – but also at various workshops in Southern and Northern Etruria – new forms of jewelry were created, such as barrel-shaped earrings, disk earrings and rings with an oval mounting and animal scenes. Like the Tarquinian painters, eastern Greek gem cutters set up their shops in southern districts of Etruria, offering their skilled workmanship to the aristocracy. Gems, chiefly carnelian, thus became status symbols. They were also used as seals and were mounted on gold rings so that the stones could turn.

162 - THIS NECKLACE IS COMPOSED OF A GOLD CORD AND A PENDANT WITH THE HEAD OF ACHELOUS. THE FIGURE'S HAIR WAS CRAFTED WITH FINE WIRES. HIS FACE, HORNS AND EARS WERE MADE WITH THE REPOUSSÉ TECHNIQUE, AND HIS BEARD WITH GRAINING. THE NECKLACE DATES TO THE EARLY 5TH CENTURY BC (LOUVRE MUSEUM, PARIS).

162-163 - THIS NECKLACE IS MADE OF CHAINS THAT FORM DIAMONDS AND TRIANGLES THAT ARE DECORATED WITH A SERIES OF GOLD PENDANTS. THE PENDANTS – THE HEAD OF ACHELOUS, HARPIES WITH OPEN WINGS, ACORNS AND LOTUS BLOSSOMS – ARE SET WITH CONTRASTING ONYX AND AMBER OVALS. THE NECKLACE DATES TO THE FIRST HALF OF THE 5TH CENTURY BC (LOUVRE MUSEUM, PARIS).

163 TOP LEFT - THE GOLD BOSS IS DECORATED WITH THE FIGURE OF A SATYR (VILLA GIULIA NATIONAL ETRUSCAN MUSEUM, ROME).

163 TOP RIGHT - THE GOLD DISK EARRING WITH CONCENTRIC MOTIFS IS MADE USING FILIGREE AND GRANULATION TECHNIQUES (BRITISH MUSEUM, LONDON).

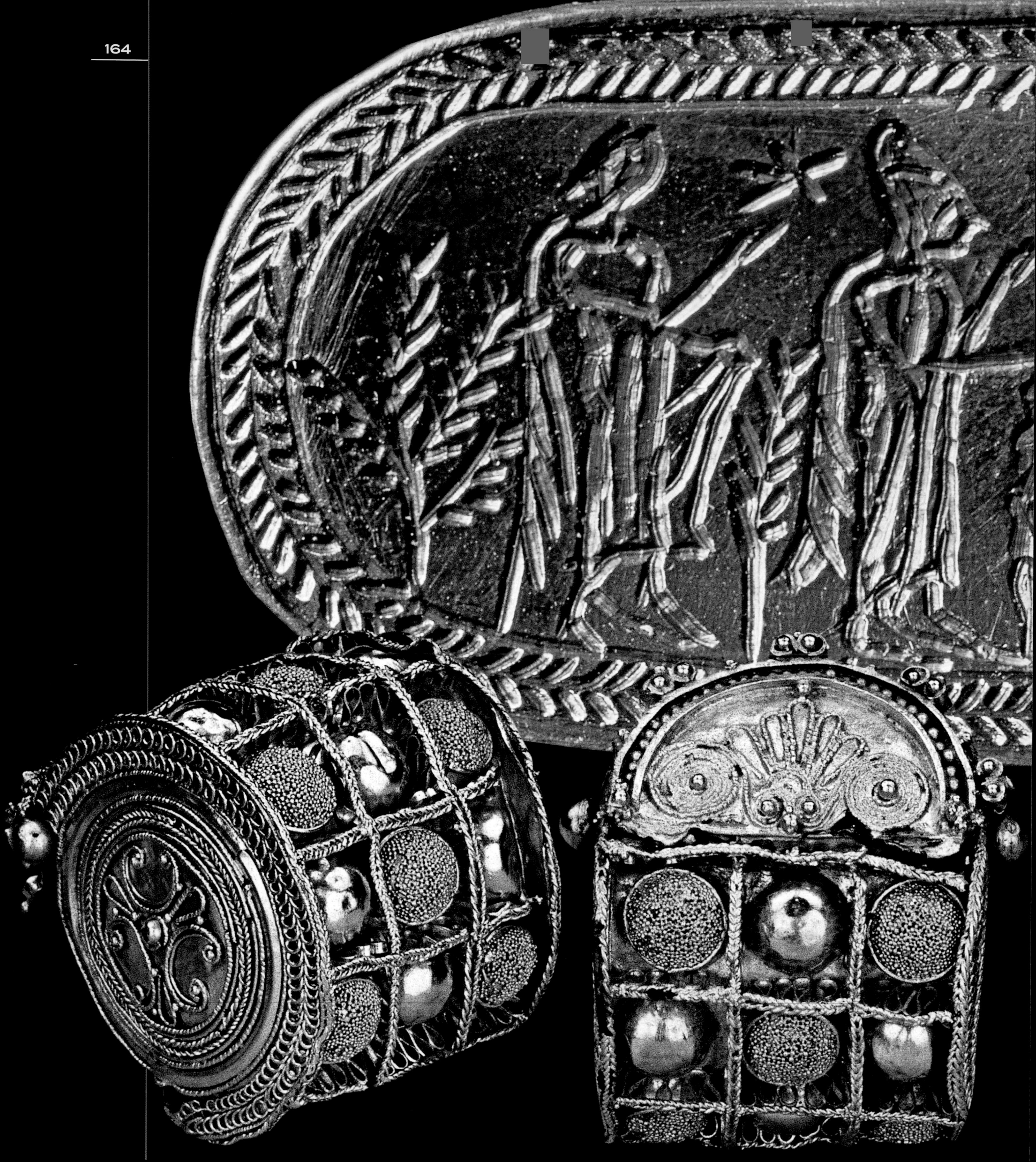

164-165 - The large setting of a
gold hollow cylinder ring has an
intaglio decoration representing
what may be a cult scene with human
figures and animals, as well as
several landscape elements, such
as a fountain, trees and stars. It is
from Cerveteri and dates to the
late 6th century BC (Villa Giulia
National Etruscan Museum, Rome).

164 bottom - This pair of
barrel-shaped earrings is
decorated with smooth beads
and grains set to create a
checkerboard motif;
filigreed plant motifs decorate
the sides. The jewelry was made
in the second half of the
6th century BC (Louvre
Museum, Paris).

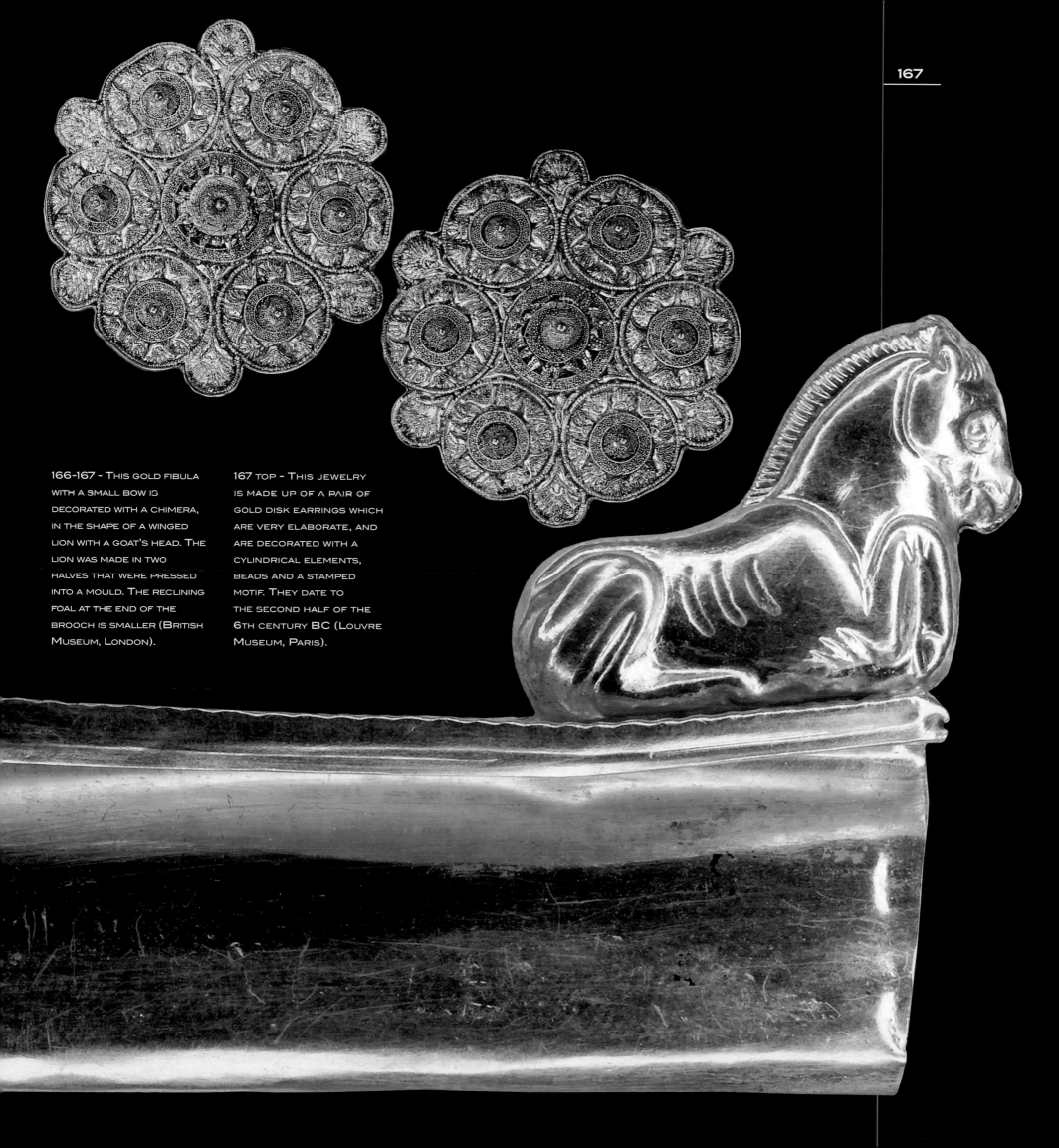

166-167 - THIS GOLD FIBULA WITH A SMALL BOW IS DECORATED WITH A CHIMERA, IN THE SHAPE OF A WINGED LION WITH A GOAT'S HEAD. THE LION WAS MADE IN TWO HALVES THAT WERE PRESSED INTO A MOULD. THE RECLINING FOAL AT THE END OF THE BROOCH IS SMALLER (BRITISH MUSEUM, LONDON).

167 TOP - THIS JEWELRY IS MADE UP OF A PAIR OF GOLD DISK EARRINGS WHICH ARE VERY ELABORATE, AND ARE DECORATED WITH A CYLINDRICAL ELEMENTS, BEADS AND A STAMPED MOTIF. THEY DATE TO THE SECOND HALF OF THE 6TH CENTURY BC (LOUVRE MUSEUM, PARIS).

5

THE PERIOD OF DECLINE: CHANGE AND ROMANIZATION

Political Forms and
the New Territorial Organization
page 170

The Aristocracy:
Earthly Life in the Afterworld
page 180

New Patronage:
Crafts and Products
page 196

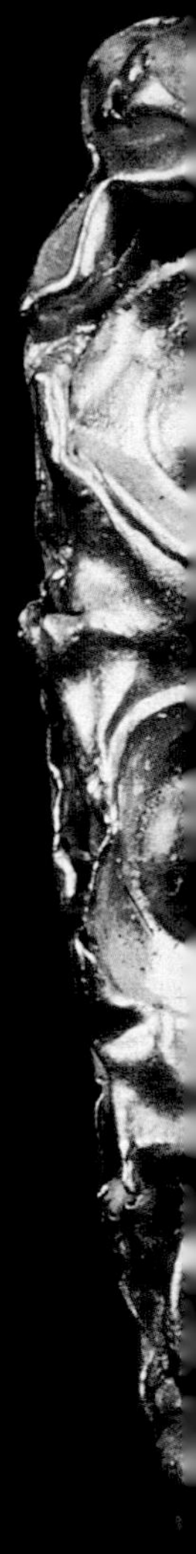

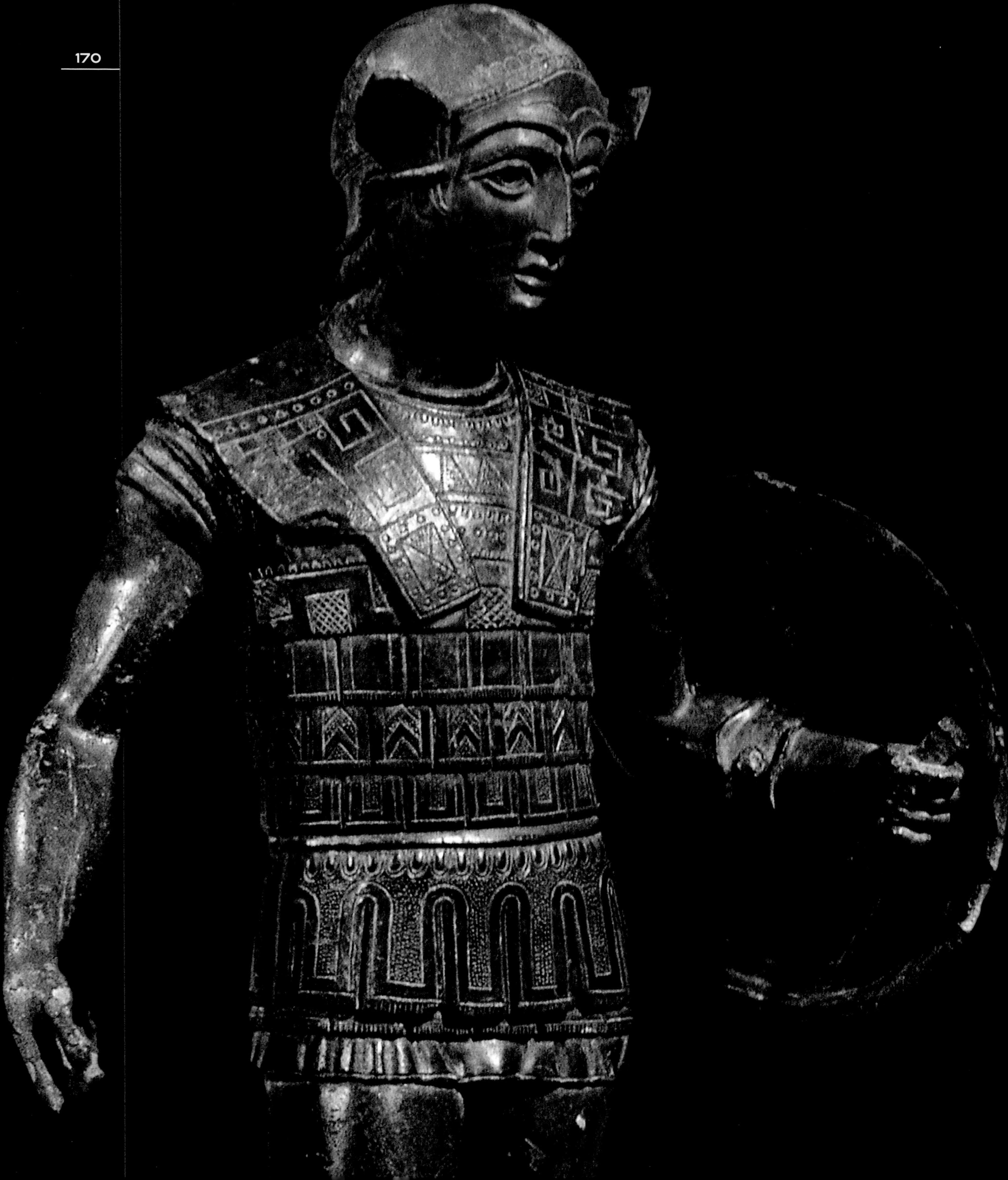

The period between the late 5th and early 4th centuries, which was fraught with crisis and substantial economic and political difficulties, culminated with the Roman conquest of Veii in 396 BC, which dealt the first blow to the aristocracy. However, the oligarchies of the Southern Etrurian cities did not accept this defeat passively and attempted to organize the coordinated reaction of several Etruscan *populi* against Rome. Tarquinia, for example, headed the opposition and, relying also on aristocratic allies, in 358 it entered into a long war that did not end until 351, when a forty-year truce was signed.

In addition to organizing an offensive against burgeoning Roman power, the aristocracy also had to consolidate its power in the face of strong social and economic tension. First of all, it replaced the traditional values on which it had founded its supremacy during the Archaic period with new ideological instruments, exploiting the magisterial power conferred by political and administrative positions.

The aristocrats also understood that it was essential to change the relationship between big cities and their outlying areas, establishing smaller centers to defend against attacks by the Roman army. At the same time, these towns offered an alternative to emerging aristocratic groups that wanted to occupy more prestigious positions. As a result, a new model of territorial organization was created, in which a large city ruled over a vast area dotted with smaller settlements, which in turn were governed by aristocratic families from the dominant city.

This new type of political and territorial organization allowed some of the cities of Southern Etruria to revive their economic activities significantly. In turn, this promoted craftsmanship, with the production of large numbers of items and livelier trade.

169 - THIS GOLD BOSS FROM SPINA IS DECORATED WITH THE FIGURE OF A YOUNG MAN REPRESENTING THE TWO-FACED GOD JANUS (ARCHAEOLOGICAL MUSEUM, FERRARA).

170 - THIS BRONZE STATUETTE DEPICTS A MAN WITH A HOPLITE'S PANOPLY (BRITISH MUSEUM, LONDON).

171 - THE BRONZE FIGURINE OF A WARRIOR WITH A HELMET WAS MADE BY A WORKSHOP IN CHIUSI IN THE MID-6TH CENTURY BC. IT IS FROM A VOTIVE DEPOSIT DISCOVERED IN BROLIO, IN THE CHIANA VALLEY (ARCHAEOLOGICAL MUSEUM, FLORENCE).

172 AND 174-175 - THIS LID FROM A BRONZE URN BEARS THE FIGURE OF THE DECEASED IN A SEMI-RECLINING POSITION, AS HE OFFERS AN OBJECT. IT IS FROM A PERUGIA TOMB DATING BACK TO THE FIRST HALF OF THE 4TH CENTURY BC. THE MODELING OF THE BODY AND THE RENDERING OF THE GARMENT COVERING THE FIGURE'S LEGS REFLECT THE STYLE OF CLASSICAL GREEK SCULPTURE (THE HERMITAGE, ST. PETERSBURG).

173 - THIS TERRACOTTA HIGH RELIEF DECORATED THE PEDIMENT OF THE TEMPLE OF THE ARA DELLA REGINA IN TARQUINIA. THE EXTANT FRAGMENTS DEPICT TWO MARVELOUS WINGED HORSES, RENDERED WITH EXTRAORDINARY ANATOMICAL DETAIL. THE WORK DATES TO THE MID-4TH CENTURY BC AND IS ONE OF THE MOST IMPORTANT ETRUSCAN SCULPTURES EVER FOUND (ARCHAEOLOGICAL MUSEUM, TARQUINIA).

The circulation of new resources in urban areas is clearly demonstrated by the resumption of intense building activity. Sanctuaries and temples were restructured and highly skilled workers were commissioned to complete decorative cycles, a trend that can be connected with the significance that the aristocracy attached to religion and ideology. Renovations such as the work done on the enormous urban sanctuary of the Ara della Regina (Altar of the Queen) in Tarquinia, with one of the rarest and most striking examples of terracotta high relief, depicting a pair of winged horses, was unquestionably promoted and managed by the ruling class as a way to express the highest level of both religious and political ideology.

Moreover, substantial transformations have been documented in the Tarquinia area, in which new settlements were established or existing ones were reconstructed over the sites of Archaic centers. Tuscania, Norchia, Castel d'Asso, San Giuliano and Ferento formed a dense network of towns that were ruled by the metropolis, and they developed a complex social stratification composed of new families or offshoots of old Tarquinian aristocratic families.

Tuscania is emblematic of the structure and importance of the smaller centers. The site prospered thanks to its fortunate position at the point where the route that paralleled the coast – which later became the Via Clodia – intersected with the one from Tarquinia that followed the Marta River and led to Lake Bolsena, Orvieto and the upper Tiber valley. In short, Tuscania was at the crossroads between the coast and the interior.

Tuscania's enormous prosperity is demonstrated by the discovery of large hypogea (underground tombs) that be-

longed to the *Curuna* family. The subterranean chambers have yielded numerous sarcophagi, accompanied by a wide variety of materials distinguished by their qality and beauty, including a group of objects inscribed with the names of their owners and probably created specifically as tomb furnishings. The case of the *gens Curuna* also provides fascinating insight into the social transformations underway in Etruria during this period, as entire family groups moved from the metropolises to smaller cities. Epigraphic documentation demonstrates that the *Curuna*, who came from an emerging Tarquinian family, rapidly became influential in Tuscania.

Another aspect tied to the renewed prosperity of Etruscan cities during the 4th century BC can be found in the organization of monetary instruments, which were not widely used previously. Given the revival of trade, however, they took on a different role. Coins minted with different standards, such as the boar, have been found, but it has also been possible to identify a figure who had a role in creating Tarquinia's coinage. This was the owner of the Giglioli Tomb, a member of the *gens Pinie* who wanted to commemorate his family in a painted frieze. This work creates the illusion of shields hanging on the walls, in the middle of which are emblems that evoke the symbols on the coins issued by the city.

Tarquinia's political and territorial model was embraced by Vulci to some extent. The territory was organized around the ruling city, which controlled several minor settlements such as Regisvilla and Ghiaccio Forte. Here as well, Vulci's brilliant economic recovery is clearly demonstrated by the existence of flourishing production activities and the appearance of new hypogea owned by the leading aristocratic families.

With the turn of the 3rd century BC, the line of resistance and offensive against Rome moved to the cities of Inland and Northern Etruria, such as Orvieto, Perugia and Arezzo, whose oligarchies managed to ally the Samnites, the Umbri and even the Gauls as a way to reopen hostilities. These harsh and bloody battles — the first waged at Sentinum in 295 BC and the second near Lake Vadimo in 283 BC — were unsuccessful, however, and culminated in the sack and destruction of Orvieto in 265 BC, after which the city's few survivors moved to what is now Bolsena. Unsatisfied, the Romans plundered the sanctuaries and took away 2000 statues in triumph, with the *evocatio* – "call to Rome" – of *Vertumnus*, the great deity who was the guardian of the confederation of the populations of Etruria, which was thus dissolved forever.

From this moment on, like the cities of Southern Etruria before them, those of Inland Etruria — no longer united and, indeed, the mirror of a disjointed population — were defeated one by one. The Etruscan political, economic and social structure gradually dissolved, as it had become completely inadequate to deal with the new economic and military dynamics of Italy and the Mediterranean. In just over a decade after the capture of Veii, Rome managed to erase Etruscan power from the peninsula's political map.

However, the different treatment that the Romans reserved for the cities of Southern and Northern Etruria allowed the latter to establish a new urban and territorial organization, albeit in different ways.

Whereas the Romans essentially confiscated half of the territory of the cities of Southern Etruria, in Northern Etruria their victory was paid off with money, helping to reinforce the ruling oligarchies. Through an intricate network of alliances and marriages, these oligarchies assured the survival of the Etruscan cities and thus their own, laying the groundwork for entry into Roman society.

In Volterra, for example, extensive restructuring work was done on the acropolis and necropolis, and numerous settlements were established for defensive purposes. Inversely, at Chiusi the population fled to the countryside, leading to an 80 percent increase in the number of sites dotting the territory and effectively parceling out arable land. Similarly, suburban settlements were organized in the countryside around Perugia.

Coins appeared in various cities of North-central Etruria in the 3rd century BC, such as the bronze series from Volterra and Populonia. They were closely related to population growth and thus crafts, and later to the payment of troops.

The aristocracies thus became allied with Rome and were increasingly integrated in Roman society. This is demonstrated not only by a series of bilingual funerary inscriptions, in which the Etruscan onomastic formulae were listed alongside the official ones of Roman cities, but also by

the adoption of forms typical of the Central Italic peninsula, such as the use of celebratory or honorary statues, the most famous is which is the Arringatore.

The attitude of the aristocracy rapidly impoverished the middle and lower classes, which were forced to seek alternatives to situations that had become unacceptable. They preferred to become mercenaries or flee to distant lands, an option chosen by many members of the lowest classes, who did not want to become part of the Roman latifundium and slave systems.

One of the "mysteries" that seems to shroud Etruscan history – its sudden "demise" – must thus be viewed instead as the slow and gradual disappearance of a way of production and a socioeconomic structure. This led to the transformation of a ruling Mediterranean nation into an area of Italy that became fully a part of the Roman world, thanks also to the fact that the Etruscans were granted Roman citizenship in 90 BC.

176 - THE STATUE KNOWN AS THE ARRINGATORE DEPICTS A MIDDLE-AGED MAN NAMED AULUS METELLUS WITH HIS RIGHT ARM RAISED TO CALL FOR SILENCE BEFORE ADDRESSING THE CROWD. IT WAS FOUND IN THE TOWN OF PILA, NEAR MODERN PERUGIA, AND DATES TO THE EARLY 1ST CENTURY BC (ARCHAEOLOGICAL MUSEUM, FLORENCE).

177 - THIS CAST BRONZE COIN WAS ISSUED BY THE CITY OF VOLTERRA IN THE 3RD CENTURY BC: THE FRONT DEPICTS THE HEAD OF THE GOD CULSANS (TWO-FACED JANUS), WHEREAS THE LEGEND OF VELATHRI IS ON THE REVERSE (ARCHAEOLOGICAL MUSEUM, VOLTERRA).

178 AND 179 - THE DECORATION ON THE
PEDIMENT OF THE TEMPLE AT TALAMONE
PORTRAYS THE MYTH OF THE SEVEN
AGAINST THEBES. THIS TERRACOTTA WORK
DATES BACK TO THE MID-2ND CENTURY

BC. IN THE CLOSE-UP, A FURY AND A
DEMON LEAD THE HORSES PULLING
AMPHIARAUS' CHARIOT (RIGHT),
DRAGGING HIM INTO THE UNDERWORLD
(ARCHAEOLOGICAL MUSEUM, FLORENCE).

THE ARISTOCRACY: EARTHLY LIFE IN THE AFTERWORLD

From the 4th to the 2nd century BC, metropolitan aristocrats played a leading role in society and politics, and their attitudes and choices marked the history of this long final phase of the Etruscan culture.

The aristocratic ideology in this important historical period was not limited to the display of luxury and opulence as in the past, but also encompassed family prestige, the importance of magisterial offices and control over religious aspects, as the nobles could interpret the mysterious will of the gods through haruspicy.

As always, the aristocracy promoted the production of top-quality goods intended strictly for their own consumption. Through them, all of these ideological elements were proposed for the dual purpose of underscoring the family's role and prestige and, with regard to the outside world, i.e., Rome, to create a special channel for political communication and an instrument to penetrate the new center of power.

In the painted tombs of the 4th century, which had decreased in number and were the privilege of a small ruling class, the traditional banquet iconography was juxtaposed with the theme of the afterlife. The underworld, which had formerly been treated metaphorically, was explicitly represented at this point, and infernal deities, the heroes of the Greek sagas and ancestors played a direct role in the ceremony. The tomb owners and their families, richly garbed and wearing jewelry, were identified by long inscriptions listing their names as well as their magisterial titles. The infernal monsters portrayed alongside them emphasized the dramatic change that had occurred in the approach towards the hereafter, in which a Hades filled with cruel and implacable demons reflected a view of life veiled by dark premonitions.

Some of the famous tombs at Tarquinia are emblematic of the mentalities of the high-standing patrons for whom they were made. For example, in the Tomb of Orcus (I and II), the deceased couple, depicted at a banquet in a Hades populated with heroes, was surrounded by evident signs of power, such as the table set with golden dinnerware. Interestingly, however, the cupbearer was a young demon. In the Tomb of the Shields, a large frieze praised the glories of the family, presenting several generations. In this case, the traditional banquet scene was smaller in order to leave room for a new theme: the procession of the magistrate. It was in this role that the deceased, accompanied by his family, presented himself to the afterworld with lictors, musicians and servants, illustrating his role and rank, and thereby projecting his real-life status into the underworld.

Another marvelous example of this type of figuration comes from the Bruschi Tomb in Tarquinia, datable to the first half of the 3rd century BC. Its walls portrayed several processions in which a larger male figure represented the deceased. Accompanied by flute players and lictors, he was welcomed by his parents and grandparents, and a son who had died as a child. The composition of the processions leaves no doubt as to the prestigious position the man held in the city administration, and he maintained this role in his journey to the afterlife. The women's names are also interesting, because they indicate their provenance – Tarquinia, Vulci and possibly Chiusi – and thus allow us to understand how extensive aristocratic alliances were during this period.

The procession scene was not part of the Greek world and can undoubtedly be considered a figuration that arose locally, perhaps for public rather than funerary use. It was one of the last creations advanced by the Etruscan aristocracy and would become part of Roman art, in which it would be incorporated into magnificent figurative cycles such as the friezes on the Ara Pacis.

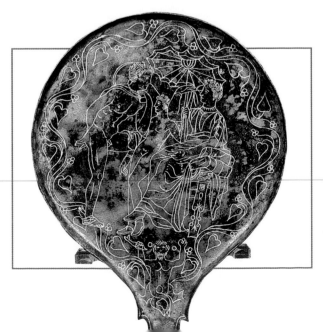

180 - IN THE 4TH CENTURY BC, SEVERAL OBJECTS DESTINED FOR THE ARISTOCRACY, SUCH AS BRONZE MIRRORS DECORATED WITH SCENES ILLUSTRATING MYTHOLOGICAL EPISODES, BEGAN TO CIRCULATE IN ETRURIA. THIS ONE IS FROM PALESTRINA AND DATES TO THE 4TH CENTURY BC (VILLA GIULIA NATIONAL ETRUSCAN MUSEUM, ROME).

181 - THIS CLOSE-UP OF THE RIGHT WALL OF THE TOMB OF ORCUS I SHOWS THE PROFILE OF THE DECEASED, VELIA, A WEALTHY WOMAN WITH ELABORATELY COIFED HAIR, A CROWN AND LAVISH JEWELRY. THE TOMB, WHICH BELONGED TO A POWERFUL ARISTOCRATIC FAMILY FROM TARQUINIA, WAS BUILT IN THE FIRST HALF OF THE 4TH CENTURY BC.

182-183 - THE TOMB OF THE ALCOVE AT CERVETERI HAS A ROOM WITH A ROOF, SUSTAINED BY SQUARE FLUTED COLUMNS.

183 TOP - THE HYPOGEUM OF THE VOLUMNI BELONGED TO A FAMILY THAT WAS PART OF PERUGIA'S LANDED ARISTOCRACY.

183 CENTER - THE TOMB OF THE BAS-RELIEFS AT CERVETERI HAS STUCCO REPRODUCTIONS OF THE FURNISHINGS USED IN AN ARISTOCRATIC HOUSEHOLD OF THE 4TH CENTURY BC.

183 BOTTOM - THE FRESCO FROM THE GOLINI TOMB I IN ORVIETO, DEPICTS THREE FIGURES PREPARING A BANQUET (ARCHAEOLOGICAL MUSEUM, ORVIETO).

Other aspects of the concept of the aristocratic tomb as an honorary monument are revealed by the decoration of the François Tomb, the only large painted hypogeum remaining at the Vulci necropolis. It masterfully illustrates the Etruscans' feelings towards Roman military and political pressure in the second half of the 4th century BC. This enormous pictorial cycle extolled the glory of the aristocratic family in a grandiose alle-

gory juxtaposing Vulci and Rome, paralleled by the portrayal of Greek heroes and the Trojans. The figurative program followed a specific logic, in which the various frescoed areas along the walls were set in relation to each other, with the figures and heroes of the Homeric cycle flanking figures and moments inspired by real events. The scenes of a local saga, referring to episodes that had occurred at least two centuries earlier in which the members of a coalition of cities – including Rome – succumbed to the blows of Vulcian heroes, were mirrored by the Homeric episode of the sacrifice of the Trojan prisoners, killed by the Greeks. All of these events were played out before the owner of the tomb, *Vel Saties*, who was taking the auspices, aided by a boy, and observed the flight of the woodpecker in order to divine the will of the gods. The intention was thus to celebrate the patron's valor during an essentially anti-Roman period, i.e., the mid-4th century BC, that was distinguished by profound conflict between Rome and some of the main Etruscan cities. Large new aristocratic tombs were rare during the 3rd century BC, but became fashionable again in the 2nd century, in which they were generally built with a single large vault designed to hold several generations of those who still considered themselves part of the aristocracy. Pictorial decoration alluded exclusively to the afterworld, in which long inscriptions were all that identified these patrons, who still tend-

ed to display the position they had held in life. In this period, the walls and pillars were predominantly decorated with large demonical figures whose increasingly menacing presence accompanied the procession of the dead. The two gigantic anguipedes (snake-like forms), painted in bright blue in the Tomb of the Typhon at Tarquinia, are notable examples.

184 TOP AND 185 BOTTOM - THE FRIEZE FROM THE FRANÇOIS TOMB DEPICTS A GREEK MOTIF, AND REAL AND MYTHICAL ANIMALS (VILLA ALBANI, ROME).

184 BOTTOM - THE FIGURE OF NESTOR WAS PAINTED IN THE FRANÇOIS TOMB.

184-185 - THE PAINTING IN THE FRANÇOIS TOMB PORTRAYS THE VULCIANS AND THEIR ALLIES, INCLUDING MASTARNA (THE FUTURE KING OF ROME, SERVIUS TULLIUS), DUELING WITH FIGURES INDICATED BY THEIR ETHNIC PROVENANCE (VILLA ALBANI, ROME).

In the 4th century BC aristocrats began to commission high-quality sarcophagi, astonishing numbers of which filled their hypogea. The first half of the 4th century BC was distinguished by highly prized ones fashioned from Greek marble by Greek or extremely Hellenized craftsmen and decorated with polychrome paintings; the famous Amazon Sarcophagus is an excellent example. However, they were rapidly replaced by sarcophagi made of local stone, in which the lid, shaped like a pitched roof, and the smooth coffins evoked wooden prototypes.

However, the 4th century BC also saw the introduction of the figure of the deceased reclining on the lid. Towards the end of the century, the figures were portrayed in the semi-reclining pose that became typical of this entire production until the 2nd century BC.

The deceased was depicted on a *kline* (couch) in a typical symposium position, holding a *patera* for libations. This clearly alluded to his or her participation at banquets, which had long been the symbol of high rank. The figures were archetypal: male and female, young or old. Their faces could be wrinkled or smooth, their hair carefully rendered or represented with just a few lines. In short, they were never true portraits. The social status of the deceased was underscored by his or her clothing and jewelry, which adorned female figures in particular, and by inscriptions bearing the name of the family, in some cases followed by the magisterial positions held by the deceased.

Over time, the portrayal of the deceased evolved based on the ideology of the period. In an early phase, male figures were depicted bare-chested, wearing only a mantle,

186-187 - The picture shows a series of terracotta sarcophagus lids. The deceased — both men and women — are depicted as they recline during a banquet. Their faces convey the artist's desire to create a portrait, but their bodies show little plasticity (Archaeological Museum, Tarquinia).

187 top and center - These close-ups show some of the paintings on the Amazon Sarcophagus, a marble item imported from Greece and found at Tarquinia. The frieze depicts the battle between the Amazons and the Greek heroes (Archaeological Museum, Tarquinia).

whereas in later portrayals the figures donned a tunic and mantle, a difference that evidently indicated a change in custom. The sarcophagus of *Laris Pulena*, made in the 2nd century BC, is a work of exceptional quality that must have been specially commissioned, given the fact that the portrait seems to have been personalized to some extent. Nevertheless, the most interesting feature is the gesture of the deceased, who is holding an open scroll to display a long inscription listing his genealogy, his work as a writer of haruspicy books, and some of the positions he held in Tarquinia, possibly in relation to the cult of Bacchus: in short, the family and roles in life that had brought him to the top of the social scale.

The sarcophagi with female figures are equally interesting, displaying intricate clothing and sumptuous jewelry. For example, the alabaster sarcophagus of *Hasti Afunei*, from the

2nd century BC, depicts the deceased stretched out on a richly decorated *kline* that has a backrest with scrolls and a pile of pillows. Her extremely elegant garb is rendered with great detail, as is her jewelry, a torque around her neck and a lavish necklace with seven bullae pendants displaying various types of workmanship.

On the sarcophagus holding the body of *Larthia Seianthi*, the terracotta workmanship exquisitely details her figure, elegant garb and jewelry, which are also underscored by rich polychrome paint. As we can see from the female figures – and, in some cases, the men – portrayed in wall paintings or on sarcophagus lids, the use of jewelry was widespread during this period. However, this custom had always distinguished the Etruscan elites, and the Orientalizing phase marked its zenith.

BELONGED TO LARTHIA
SEIANTI. IT IS DISTINGUISHED
BY ITS RICH POLYCHROME
DECORATION AND THE FINE
DETAILING OF THE
GARMENTS, THE WOMAN'S
ORNAMENTS, THE KLINE AND
THE FLORAL DECORATION ON
THE CASKET. THIS OBJECT,
WHICH BELONGED TO A
MEMBER OF CHIUSI'S
ARISTOCRACY, DATES BACK
TO THE FIRST HALF OF THE
2ND CENTURY BC
(ARCHAEOLOGICAL
MUSEUM, FLORENCE).

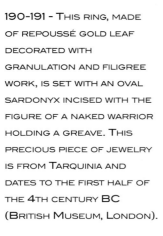

190-191 - This ring, made of repoussé gold leaf decorated with granulation and filigree work, is set with an oval sardonyx incised with the figure of a naked warrior holding a greave. This precious piece of jewelry is from Tarquinia and dates to the first half of the 4th century BC (British Museum, London).

191 - This brooch, made of double gold leaf, is decorated with rows of beads divided by filigree cords that end in a palmette with 11 petals. This rare object is from a tomb at the Spina necropolis and dates to the early 4th century BC (Archaeological Museum, Ferrara).

Starting in the 4th century BC, jewelry reflected rather lavish tastes, as can be seen from the cluster earrings that were gradually embellished with increasingly elaborate decorations, as well as simple tubular earrings ending in an animal head. The bulla is frequently seen in figurations. This object, composed of two hemispheres, held aromatic substances. Bullae were decorated with repoussé work or stamped with mythological scenes, some of which very complex. In some cases, they were part of heavy necklaces that, as an alternative, could also have different kinds of pendants.

During this period, it became fashionable for aristocratic men and women alike to wear gold wreaths on their heads.

At the end of the 4th century BC, when new trends that had become popular among Macedonian aristocrats reached Etruria through contacts with Magna Graecia, artisans merged local and Greek traditions, producing jewelry that revived abandoned techniques such as filigree and granulation. These techniques were used for different objects, particularly earrings with multiform and pyramid pendants, which would remain in vogue until the end of the 2nd century BC.

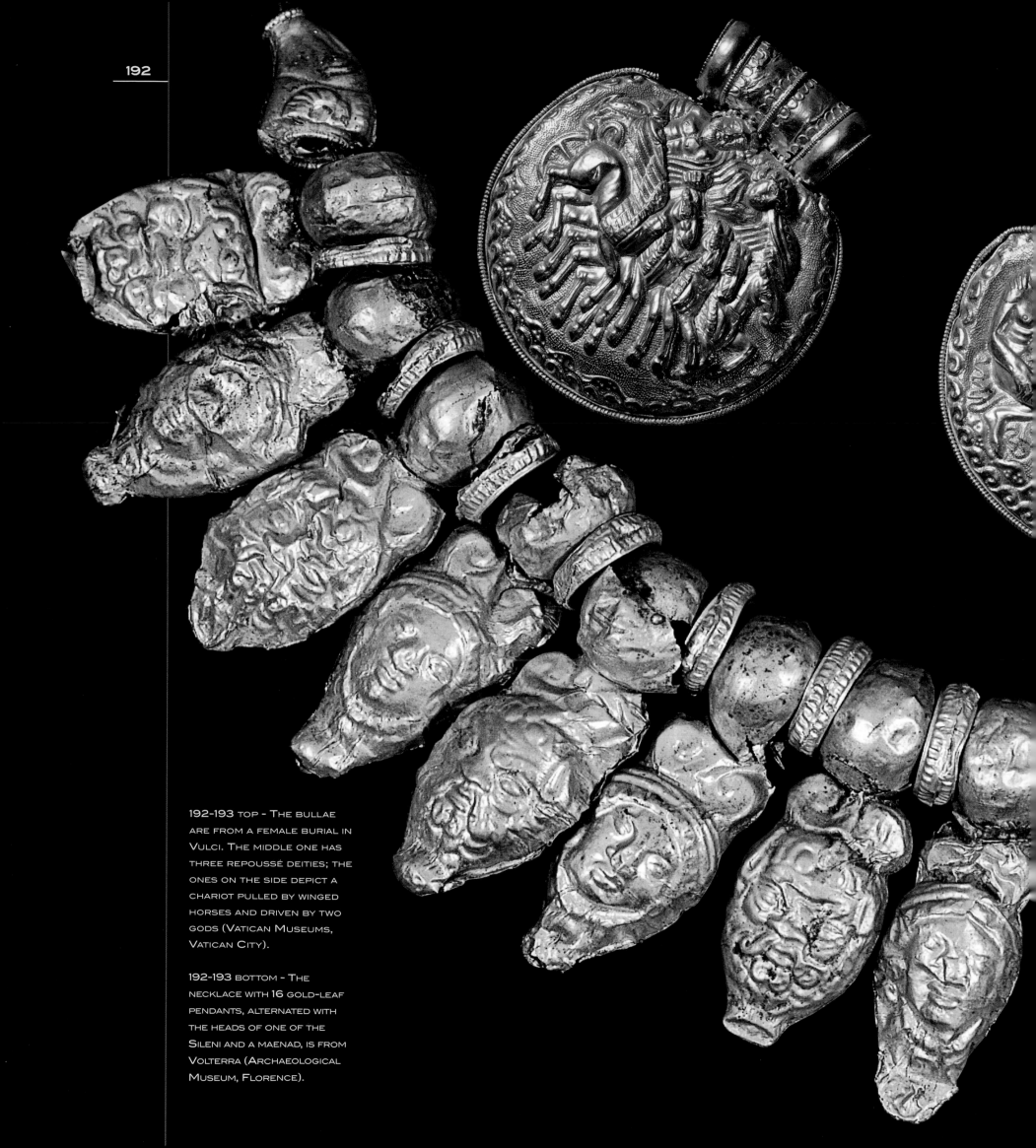

192-193 top - The bullae
are from a female burial in
Vulci. The middle one has
three repoussé deities; the
ones on the side depict a
chariot pulled by winged
horses and driven by two
gods (Vatican Museums,
Vatican City).

192-193 bottom - The
necklace with 16 gold-leaf
pendants, alternated with
the heads of one of the
Sileni and a maenad, is from
Volterra (Archaeological
Museum, Florence).

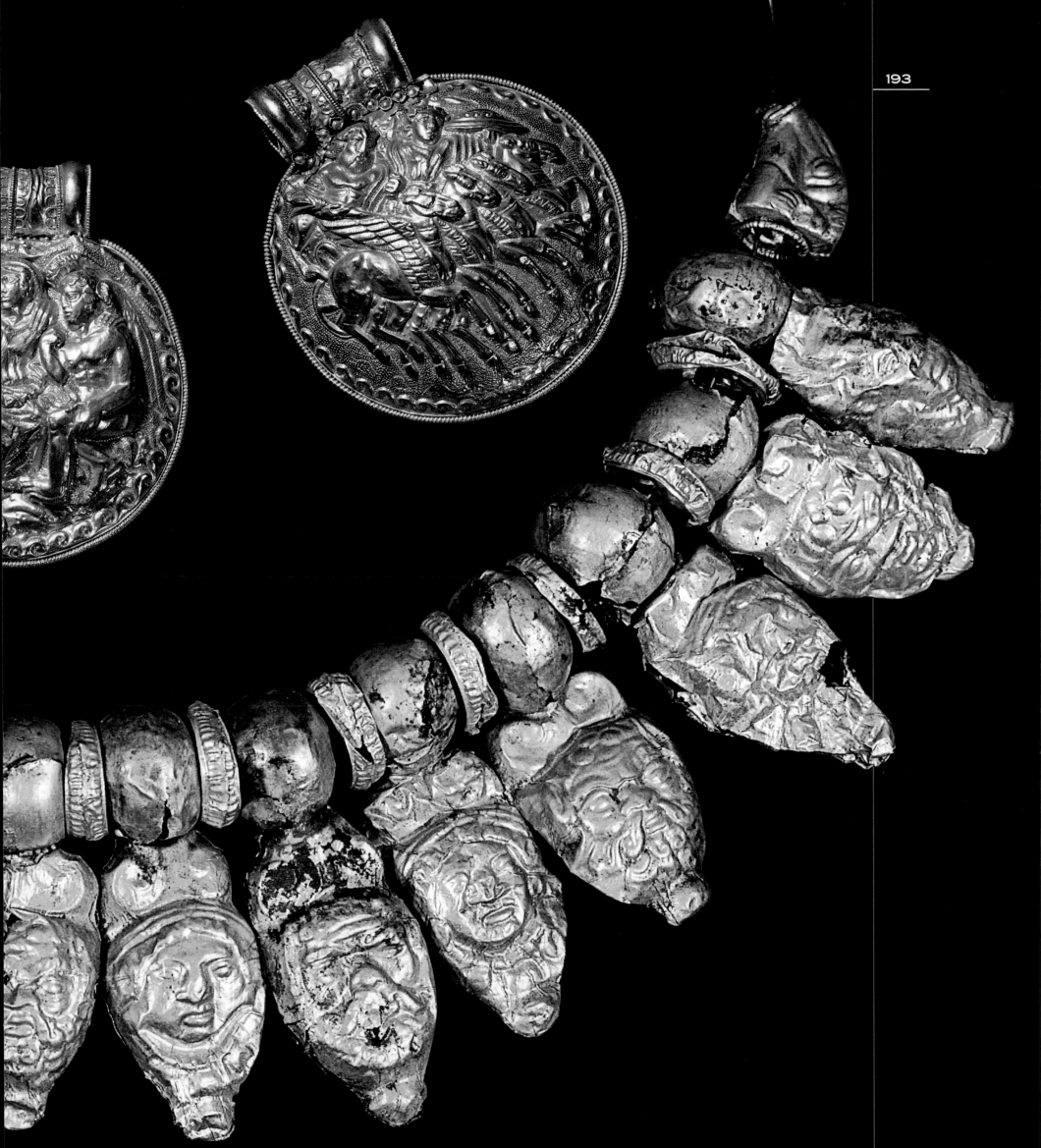

194 - THE PENDANTS ON THESE TWO
GOLD EARRINGS FROM TODI (ANCIENT
TUDER; LEFT) AND CERVETERI (RIGHT)
PORTRAY A WOMAN'S HEAD AND AN
AMPHORA (VILLA GIULIA NATIONAL
ETRUSCAN MUSEUM, ROME).

195 - THIS NECKLACE FROM TODI
HAS TWO GOLD BULLAE. ONE
IS STAMPED WITH A WOMAN'S HEAD,
AND THE OTHER IS SET WITH AN ONYX
(VILLA GIULIA NATIONAL ETRUSCAN
MUSEUM, ROME).

In the 4th century BC, the renewed prosperity of several cities helped revive economic processes, with the resumption of artisanal activities, which had to cater to the new territorial organization as well as a new and more complex social structure.

In addition to aristocrats, the society of the era also had a large middle class composed of artisans and merchants who had amassed land or assets. These segments of society were gradually co-opted by the aristocracy, which evidently needed new capital. There is evidence that the members of the middle class became increasingly important during the 3rd and 2nd centuries BC and, also through marriages, were able to participate in the public administration and access positions of command in the army. The lower classes were composed of servants or former servants, tied in particular to agricultural work and thus with a limited production capacity and few financial resources. During the 3rd century and, above all, the 2nd century BC these subordinate groups were replaced by slaves, typically connected with the latifundium system. This sparked a shift towards mercenary work and settlement in other areas, in some cases far from the Mediterranean, as demonstrated by several boundary stones with Etruscan inscriptions found in Tunisia and the Liber linteus (linen book) of Zagreb, which ended up in Egypt and was used to wrap a mummy. Between the 4th and 3rd centuries BC, the middle classes and subordinate groups that had the means – however limited – to purchase consumer goods began to have a powerful impact on production, altering the balance between patronage and handicrafts.

First of all, given the fact that the new classes were willing to settle for objects per se and did not demand higher technical quality or a richer figurative repertoire, artisans were not stimulated to innovate. This led to standardization and a general decline in the level of all handicrafts. Inversely, however, due to the growing number of consumers, workshops were forced to reorganize in order to work faster. Thus, the shop head finished only the most important parts of the product and the rest was left to apprentices.

Nevertheless, these new products were well received even outside the Etruscan market, which was becoming reorganized through the creation of new trade flows for foodstuffs and goods, and the circulation of pottery, bronze artifacts and metal vessels. The cities of Southern Etruria exported goods south to Latium and north to Liguria, the south of France and the Adriatic coast; the cities of Inland Etruria exported to the Po Valley. Through Roman middlemen, Etruscan goods also traveled as far as Carthage, Malta and Rhodes.

Pottery production enjoyed a significant revival, thanks to the influx of artifacts from Attica and Magna Graecia to the Etruscan market. The quantity and quality of these products provide an excellent example of how the workshops must have been set up in order to cater to a growing and increasingly differentiated clientele, composed not only of wealthy, educated and sophisticated aristocrats accustomed to luxury goods, but also merchants, artisans and the lower classes, who were interested in purchasing goods suited to their limited cultural level and financial resources.

In the early 4th century BC, the workshops of Falerii (now Civita Castellana) and Vulci were the first to organize workshops designed to meet the demands of the aristocracy, which Attic trade was unable to satisfy. During this initial phase, large vases predominated, and their high quality indicates that they were made for luxury consumption. Their figurative repertory was represented by images of the gods and heroes, as well as the themes of love and profane amusements, subjects that were popular among the aristocracy. In the mid-4th century BC Vulcian workshops continued to cater to upper-level customers, producing vases that were closely connected with the symposium ritual. It is interesting to note that these vessels were made strictly to hold liquids – water and wine – but not to pour them. This oddity explains the existence of Vulcian workshops that produced simpula, or bronze ladles, thus making pouring vessels unnecessary.

The market during this period was so lively that the workshops of Cerveteri began to produce goods for the middle classes, as suggested by the fact that the figurative repertory included images from the Dionysian sphere and the world of women, whereas mythological themes were abandoned. Within a decade, this Caeretan production developed into the most important in Etruria, and goods were exported as far as Aleria, in Corsica.

The new customers from the Chiana valley and Volterra must also have been part of the middle class. To cater to this demand, a group of artisans – possibly Faliscans – set up a workshop in Chiusi, mainly producing cups decorated with symposiac scenes. In the mid-4th century, the workshops of Volterra, in turn, produced only red-figure kraters, which were used as cinerary urns and were thus decorated with funerary subjects. The surface of the vessel even bore a symbolic portrait of the deceased, represented solely by the head in profile. Although this production was merely of average quality, it was extremely successful in Northern Etruria, spreading to Chiusi, the Po area and even Corsica.

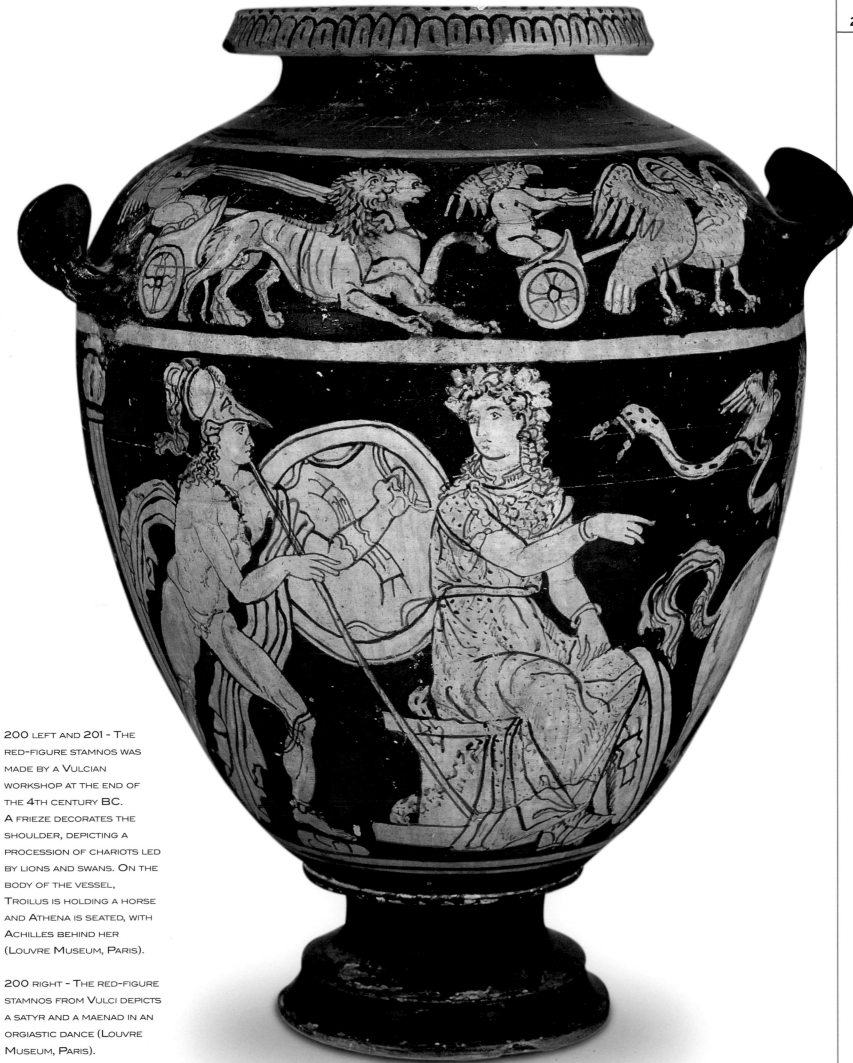

200 LEFT AND 201 - THE
RED-FIGURE STAMNOS WAS
MADE BY A VULCIAN
WORKSHOP AT THE END OF
THE 4TH CENTURY BC.
A FRIEZE DECORATES THE
SHOULDER, DEPICTING A
PROCESSION OF CHARIOTS LED
BY LIONS AND SWANS. ON THE
BODY OF THE VESSEL,
TROILUS IS HOLDING A HORSE
AND ATHENA IS SEATED, WITH
ACHILLES BEHIND HER
(LOUVRE MUSEUM, PARIS).

200 RIGHT - THE RED-FIGURE
STAMNOS FROM VULCI DEPICTS
A SATYR AND A MAENAD IN AN
ORGIASTIC DANCE (LOUVRE
MUSEUM, PARIS).

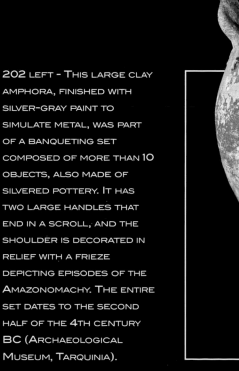

The workshops of Falerii and Cerveteri also targeted an extensive middle-class market, and in the second half of the 4th century BC they made a large number of products that were very similar in both form and iconography. These artifacts were extremely popular and were widely circulated.

Caeretan artisans grasped the potential of this large new market composed of the middle and lower classes, which wanted objects that were not connected with the aristocratic ideology. As a result, they produced enormous quantities of artifacts that were painted black with a small ghostly figure overpainted in white. These vessels – almost exclusively jugs with a beaked spout – were made by specialized workshops that had undertaken an industrial type of production. Likewise, the Genucilia plates from the late 4th century BC were highly standardized products made for the Mediterranean market.

Throughout the 3rd century, various areas and numerous workshops produced vases that were painted entirely black, with a lustrous surface designed to imitate metal.

Among the various workshops, the Malacena factory produced high-quality artifacts, including elegant and finely wrought vases that were intended for luxury consumption and could thus be afforded only by a small number of customers. The repertory included particularly large and complex forms, with an impressed decoration made by stamping the fresh clay. Likewise, the Faliscan and Volsinian workshops made large vases for a clientele that, although demanding, had limited financial means. These artifacts were made of purified clay and were then finished with a silvery patina in order resemble silverware.

Following the territorial reorganization of the areas around Chiusi and Perugia, a large number of people from the lower classes occupied small settlements that dotted vast agricultural areas. Between the 3rd and 2nd centuries BC, rather modest products – mainly uncolored pottery that was often miniaturized – were made for these customers and accompanied unpretentious burials in small niches.

202 LEFT - THIS LARGE CLAY AMPHORA, FINISHED WITH SILVER-GRAY PAINT TO SIMULATE METAL, WAS PART OF A BANQUETING SET COMPOSED OF MORE THAN 10 OBJECTS, ALSO MADE OF SILVERED POTTERY. IT HAS TWO LARGE HANDLES THAT END IN A SCROLL, AND THE SHOULDER IS DECORATED IN RELIEF WITH A FRIEZE DEPICTING EPISODES OF THE AMAZONOMACHY. THE ENTIRE SET DATES TO THE SECOND HALF OF THE 4TH CENTURY BC (ARCHAEOLOGICAL MUSEUM, TARQUINIA).

202 RIGHT - THIS IMPRESSIVE CLAY CALYX KRATER, FINISHED IN SILVER-GRAY PAINT, IS DECORATED WITH A GRAPEVINE IN RELIEF AROUND THE BOWL. IT IS SET ON A TALL SHAPED PEDESTAL THAT EVOKES THE METAL ARTIFACTS IT WAS DESIGNED TO IMITATE (ARCHAEOLOGICAL MUSEUM, TARQUINIA).

203 - THE CLAY AMPHORA FINISHED IN SILVER-GRAY PAINT HAS TWISTED HANDLES (ARCHAEOLOGICAL MUSEUM, TARQUINIA).

INDEX

c = caption

A

Accesa, Lake 133
Acquarossa 80, 82, 83
Adria 98, 129
Allumiere 27
Apollo Master 114
Archaeological Museum, Arezzo 7c, 124c
Archaeological Museum, Athens, 23c
Archaeological Museum, Bologna, 39c, 44c,
  121c
Archaeological Museum, Capua 97c
Archaeological Museum, Ferrara 140c, 171c,
  191c
Archaeological Museum, Florence 23c, 33c,
  34c, 43c, 55c, 67c, 68c, 73c, 74c, 86c, 87c,
  123c, 128c, 138c, 171c, 177c, 178c, 188c,
  192c
Archaeological Museum, Grosseto, 35c, 43c,
  101c
Archaeological Museum, Orvieto, 107c,
  111c, 183c
Archaeological Museum, Palermo 12c, 158c
Archaeological Museum, Tarquinia 57c, 87c,
  143c, 172c, 186c, 203c
Archaeological Museum, Volterra, 33c, 35c,
  177c
Arezzo (Arretium), 176
Aristonothos krater 88, 88c
Augustus, emperor 24, 25
Aulus Metellus 177c
Aurora Painter 197c

B

Battle of Cumae 13, 102, 119, 129
Battle of Elba 13, 129
Battle of Himera 13, 102
Battle of Lake Vadimo 13, 176
Battle of Salamis 13, 102
Battle of Sentinum 13, 176
Bisenzio (Visentium) 36c, 43, 43c, 47, 48c,
  87, 88c
British Museum, London, 8c, 30c, 53c, 85c,
  95c, 97c, 102c, 134c, 143c, 162c, 163c,
  167c, 171c, 191c
Brolio 171c

C

Campano Museum, Santa Maria Capua
  Vetere 97c
Campetti, Veii 121c
Capitol, Rome 94, 95, 114
Capitoline Museums, Rome 8c
Capua 97c, 98
Castel d'Asso 172
Cato 126
Cavalupo 36c
Cerveteri (Caere) 12c, 30, 31, 38c, 59, 60c,
  61, 67c, 74, 74c, 77, 84, 85c, 87, 88, 88c,
  100, 102, 102c, 110, 118, 119, 119c, 127c,
  128, 128c, 129, 133, 133c, 134, 144, 165c,
  183c, 194c, 200, 203
Chimera of Arezzo 7c, 8, 121, 124c
Chiusi (Clusium) 31, 53c, 73c, 128c, 129, 133,
  134, 137c, 158c, 159, 177, 180, 200, 203
Civic Museum, Livorno 25c
Civita Hill, Tarquinia 47

Claudius, emperor 10
Cloaca Maxima, Rome 94
Coste del Marano 27
Critias, 138
Crostoletto di Lamone 26
Cumae 42, 84
Curia (Hostilia), Rome 94

D

Diodorus Siculus 10, 86, 133
Dionysius of Halicarnassus 8, 10, 22, 86, 133

E

Eagle Painter, 128c
Elba, island of 25
Ephorus 86
Ergotimos 129
Estense Museum, Modena 123c

F

Faina Museum, Orvieto, 109c, 113c
Falerii (Civita Castellana) 197c, 200, 203
Felsina (Bologna) 32, 39c
Ferento 172
Forum Antiquarium, Rome 92c
Forum Boarium, Rome 94c
François krater, 128c, 129

G

Genucilia plates 203
Ghiaccio Forte 172
Gozzadini, Giovanni 30
Gravisca 127c, 128

H

Hellanicus of Lesbos 22
Hermitage, St. Petersburg 140c, 172c
Herodotus 10, 22, 128
Hippodamus of Miletus, 101
Homer, 46
House of the Cryptoporticus, Vulci, 101c
House of the Impluvium, Roselle 101, 101c
House of the Oil Merchant, Mycenae, 26
Hypogeum of the Volumni 183c

K

Kerameikos, Athens 129
Kleitias 129
Kunsthistorisches Museum, Vienna 92c

L

Leonardo da Vinci 8
Liber linteus 197
Livy 10, 98
Louvre Museum, Paris 34c, 43c, 53c, 54c,
  57c, 61c, 73c, 85c, 127c, 128c, 131c, 133c,
  134c, 137c, 162c, 165c, 167c, 197c, 201c
Luni sul Mignone 26, 27, 27c

M

Malacena factory 203
Marsiliana d'Albegna 31, 67c, 73c, 84
Marzabotto 98, 98c, 101
Mezentius 85c
Micali Painter, 143, 143c
Mithraeum, Vulci 101c
Monte Acuto Ragazza 121c
Monte Amiata 25, 26

Monte Rovello 26, 27
Municipal Antiquarium, Rome 94c
Murlo 80, 80c, 81c, 82, 83
Museum of Poggio Civitate, Murlo 70c, 80c,
  81c

N

National Cerite Museum, Cerveteri 57c
Necropolis, Banditaccia, Cerveteri 76c, 77c,
  102, 102c
Necropolis, Crocefisso del Tufo, Orvieto 102
Necropolis, Monte Michele, Veii 61, 74
Necropolis, Monterozzi, Tarquinia 147c,
  148c, 154c, 155c, 156c
Necropolis, Osteria, Vulci 46
Necropolis, Poggio la Pozza 27
Necropolis, Quattro Fontanili, Veii 46
Norchia 172

O

Orientalizing culture 13, 50-89
Orvieto (Volsinii) 31, 80, 95, 102, 107c,
  109c, 113c, 133, 172, 176

P

Palatine Antiquarium, Rome 92c
Palestrina (Praeneste) 59, 60c, 61, 62c, 63c,
  68c, 70c, 73c, 180c
Pallottino, Massimo 22
Perugia (Perusia) 172c, 176, 177, 177c,
  183c, 203
Pescia Romana 43c
Piazza d'Armi, Veii 80, 100
Pila 177c
Pilgrim flask 23c
Piombino 25
Pithekoussai (Ischia) 13, 42, 84
Pliny the Elder, 10, 98, 114
Plutarch 10
Pluto, 158c
Poggio dell'Impiccato, Tarquinia 40
Poggio Selciatello, Tarquinia 32
Polybius 10
Populonia 25, 31, 34, 40, 126, 129, 133, 138,
  138c, 177
Porta Laurentina, Arezzo 124c
Puglisi, Salvatore 26
Pyrgi 100, 110, 118, 119, 119c, 128

R

Regia, Rome 94
Regisvilla 128, 172
Rome 13, 24, 86, 88, 92c, 94, 95, 98, 114,
  126, 133, 171, 176, 180, 184
Roselle 31

S

San Giovenale 27, 101c
San Giuliano 172
Sanctuary of Voltumna (Fanum Voltumnae),
  Orvieto, 95
Sanctuary, Gravisca 128
Sarcophagus of Hasti Afunei, Tarquinia 187
Sarcophagus of Laris Pulena, Tarquinia 187
Sarcophagus of Larthia Seianthi, Tarquinia
  187, 188c
Sarcophagus of the Spouses 12c, 144, 144c
Sarcophagus, Amazon, Tarquinia 186, 186c

Servius Tullius (Mastarna) 94, 184c
Simpula 200
Sorgenti della Nova 27
Sostratos 128
Spina 98, 101, 129, 171c, 191c
Statue of Apollo, Veii 117c
Statue of Mars, Todi, 121, 123c
Statue of the Arringatore 8, 177, 177c
Strabo 10, 86, 88

T
Tacitus 10
Talamone 25
Tarquinia 13, 30, 31, 32, 33c, 34c, 35, 37, 42,
  43, 54c, 57c, 80, 87, 87c, 127c, 128, 129,
  134c, 146, 147c, 150c, 152, 153c, 154c,
  155c, 156c, 162, 171, 172, 180, 180c, 186c,
  187, 191c
Tarquinius Priscus (Tarquin the Elder) 94, 114
Tarquinius Superbus (Tarquin the Proud) 94,
  95, 114
Temple A, Pyrgi 118, 119, 119c
Temple B, Pyrgi 118
Temple of Capitoline Jupiter, Rome 94, 95,
  114
Temple of Mater Matuta, Satricum 110c, 113c
Temple of Portonaccio, Veii 8c
Temple of Talamone, 178c
Temple of Via S. Leonardo, Orvieto 109c
Temple or sanctuary of Portonaccio, Veii
  92c, 110, 114, 114c, 117c, 118, 121
Temple, Ara della Regina, Tarquinia 172, 172c
Temple, Belvedere, Orvieto 109c, 111c,
  113c
Thefarie Velianas 118
Todi (Tuder) 123c, 194c
Tolfa 27
Tomb of Montescudaio 74, 74c
Tomb of Orcus I, Tarquinia 180, 180c
Tomb of Orcus II, Tarquinia 180
Tomb of the Alcove, Cerveteri 183c

Tomb of the Augurs, Tarquinia 147, 150c
Tomb of the Baron, Tarquinia 156c
Tomb of the Bas-reliefs, Cerveteri 183c
Tomb of the Bigas, Tarquinia 154
Tomb of the Bulls, Tarquinia 146, 147c
Tomb of the Chariot, Vulci 58c
Tomb of the Doli, Cerveteri 10c
Tomb of the Duce, Vetulonia 61, 87c
Tomb of the Flabella, Populonia 138c
Tomb of the Funeral Beds, Cerveteri 76c
Tomb of the Funerary Bed, Tarquinia 154
Tomb of the Hunter, Tarquinia 146
Tomb of the Ivories, Marsiliana d'Albegna 61
Tomb of the Ivories, Marsiliana d'Albegna
  73c, 84
Tomb of the Jugglers, Tarquinia 147, 150c
Tomb of the Leopards, Tarquinia 7c, 154,
  154c, 155
Tomb of the Lictor, Vetulonia 61, 68c, 74
Tomb of the Lionesses, Tarquinia 146, 147c,
  152
Tomb of the Olympiad, Tarquinia 147
Tomb of the Shields, Tarquinia 180
Tomb of the Ship, Tarquinia 154
Tomb of the Triclinium, Tarquinia 154c, 155c
Tomb of the Typhon, Tarquinia 184
Tomb of the Warrior, Vulci 138, 138c
Tomb of Verucchio 61
Tomb, Barberini, Palestrina, 7c, 61, 70c, 73c
Tomb, Bernardini, Palestrina 60c, 61, 62c,
  63c, 65c, 68c, 69c
Tomb, Bocchoris, Tarquinia 59
Tomb, Bruschi, Tarquinia 180
Tomb, Circle of the Cauldrons, Vetulonia
  55c
Tomb, Fowling and Fishing, Tarquinia 152,
  153c
Tomb, François, Vulci 184, 184c
Tomb, Giglioli, Tarquinia 172
Tomb, Golini I, Orvieto 183c
Tomb, Isis, Vulci 53c

Tomb, Pania, Chiusi, 73c
Tomb, Regolini-Galassi, Cerveteri 7c, 53c,
  61, 62c, 65c, 69c, 74, 74c, 84
Tumulus tomb of Castellina 8
Tumulus tomb of the Painted Animals,
  Cerveteri 77c
Tuscania 172

U
Urartu, kingdom of 52, 53
Urgulanilla 10

V
Vatican Museums, Vatican City 7c, 53c, 62c,
  65c, 69c, 74c, 85c, 123c, 192c
Veii 13, 30, 31, 42, 43, 45, 46, 47, 80, 84,
  92c, 100, 101, 110, 114, 114c, 121, 121d,
  133, 171, 176
Velia 180c
Velletri (Velitrae) 92c
Vetulonia 31, 32, 35c, 40, 55c, 68c, 87c, 88, 101
Via Aurelia 31
Via Cassia 31
Via Clodia 172
Via dei Monti della Tolfa, Cerveteri 102c
Villa Albani, Rome 184c
Villa Giulia National Etruscan Museum,
  Rome 7c, 8c, 10c, 12c, 23c, 30c, 36c, 38c,
  40c, 41c, 48c, 49c, 58c, 60c, 62c, 63c, 65c,
  67c, 68c, 69c, 70c, 73c, 88c, 92c, 107c,
  110c, 113c, 114c, 117c, 119c, 138c, 144c,
  163c, 165c, 180c, 194c, 197c
Villanovan culture 13, 28-49
Virgil 10
Vitruvius 106
Volcanius 114
Volterra (Volaterrae) 32, 33c, 35c, 46, 74,
  129, 177, 177c, 192c, 200
Vulci 30, 30c, 31, 32, 40c, 41, 41c, 43, 46, 49c,
  53c, 59, 101c, 107c, 128, 129, 131c, 138, 138c,
  140c, 143c, 162, 172, 180, 184, 192c, 200, 201c

BARTOLONI, GILDA. *La cultura villanoviana. All'inizio della storia etrusca*, NIS, new edition, Rome 2002.
BARTOLONI, GILDA. *Le società dell'Italia primitiva. Lo studio delle necropoli e la nascita delle aristocrazie*, Carocci, Rome 2003.
CAMPOREALE, GIOVANNANGELO (ED.). *Gli Etruschi fuori dall'Etruria*, Arsenale Editrice, Verona 2001.
COLONNA, GIOVANNI (ED.). *Santuari d'Etruria*, Electa, Florence – Milan 1985.
COLONNA, GIOVANNI. "Etrusca arte", in *Enciclopedia dell'Arte Antica*, 2nd supplement, Rome 1994.
CRISTOFANI, MAURO (ED.). *Gli Etruschi. Una nuova immagine*, Giunti, Florence 1984.
CRISTOFANI, MAURO (ED.). *I bronzi degli Etruschi*, Istituto Geografico De Agostini, Novara 1985.
CRISTOFANI, MAURO AND MARINA MARTELLI (EDS.). *L'oro degli Etruschi*, Istituto Geografico De Agostini, Novara 1983.
CRISTOFANI, MAURO. *Gli Etruschi del mare*, Longanesi, Milan 1983.
CRISTOFANI, MAURO. *L'arte degli Etruschi. Produzione e consumo*, Einaudi, Turin 1978.
Die Etrusker, Hirmer Verlag, Hamburg 2004.
Gli Etruschi, Bompiani, Venice 2000.
HAYNES, SYBILLE. *Etruscan Bronzes*, Sotheby's Publications, London 1985.
HAYNES, SYBILLE. *Etruscan Civilization: A Cultural History*, British Museum Press, London 2000.
Les Étrusques et l'Europe, Editions de la Réunion des Museés Nationaux, Paris 1992.
MACNAMARA, ELLEN. *The Etruscans*, The British Museum Press, London 1990.
MAGGIANI, ADRIANO (ED.). *Artigianato artistico in Etruria*, Electa, Florence – Milan 1985.
MARTELLI, MARINA (ED.). *La ceramica degli Etruschi. La pittura vascolare*, Istituto Geografico De Agostini, Novara 1987.
PALLOTTINO, MASSIMO. *Etruscologia*, 7th ed., Hoepli, Milan 1984.
PALLOTTINO, MASSIMO. *Origini e storia primitiva di Roma*, Rusconi, Rome 1993.
Principi etruschi tra Mediterraneo ed Europa, Marsilio, Bologna 2000.
Rasenna. Storia e civiltà degli Etruschi, Garzanti – Scheiwiller, Milan 1986.
SPIVEY, NIGEL. *Etruscan Art*, Thames and Hudson, London 1997.
STEINGRÄBER, STEPHEN (ED.). *Catalogo ragionato della pittura etrusca*, Jaca Book, Milan 1985.
TORELLI, MARIO. *L'arte degli Etruschi*, Laterza, Bari 1985.
TORELLI, MARIO. *Storia degli Etruschi*, Laterza, Bari 1981.

PHOTO CREDITS

To Federico, my beloved son.

208 - This small bronze object
from the ornament of a parade
chariot represents a sun god with
two large wings and his head
surrounded by rays; it is from
the early 5th century BC
(British Museum, London).